Thirty Classic Patchwork Patterns

DOROTHY H. WELCH

Illustrated by
Richard E. Welch

DOVER PUBLICATIONS, INC.
New York

Copyright

Copyright © 1996 by Richard E. Welch.
All rights reserved under Pan American and International Copyright Conventions.

Published in Canada by General Publishing Company, Ltd., 30 Lesmill Road, Don Mills, Toronto, Ontario.
Published in the United Kingdom by Constable and Company, Ltd., 3 The Lanchesters, 162–164 Fulham Palace Road, London W6 9ER.

Bibliographical Note

Thirty Classic Patchwork Patterns is a new work, first published by Dover Publications, Inc., in 1996.

Library of Congress Cataloging-in-Publication Data

Welch, Dorothy H.
    Thirty classic patchwork patterns / Dorothy H. Welch ; illustrated by Richard E. Welch.
        p.   cm.
    ISBN 0-486-28967-2 (pbk.)
    1. Patchwork—Patterns. 2. Patchwork quilts. I. Title.
TT835.W457   1996
746.46—dc20   95-37112
                                                                                                        CIP

Manufactured in the United States of America
Dover Publications, Inc., 31 East 2nd Street, Mineola, N.Y. 11501

Quilt Making Basics

Quilting Terms–

Appliqué —
A technique whereby a cut out foreground piece(s) of fabric (the appliqué) is sewn onto a larger background piece (sometimes called the ground or base).

Backing —
The back fabric of the quilt that provides for a neat finish, and is the bottom layer of the three quilt layers: top, batting, and backing.

Backstitch —
A backwards direction stitch used to reinforce and secure the seam stitches; taken at both the beginning and end of a seam.

Basting —
Large, temporary running stitches used to hold the quilt's layers together, or to hold an appliqué to its background. They are removed after the permanent, tightly placed stitches are in place. When basting is used to hold the three layers of the quilt together for the final quilting, they are sewn in a loose grid pattern across the entire quilt—working from the center out.

Batting —
The middle layer of the quilt used to add texture and bulk. The bulk makes for a much warmer quilt, but be careful not to use too thick a batting as it is too difficult to quilt, and must be tied. Conversely, too thin a batting is hard to keep in place unless the quilting stitches are quite close together. This means a great deal of extra quilting to firmly hold the batting in position. A medium batting, on the other hand, is easy to quilt and stays in position rather well. Medium thickness batting is what is recommended for the projects in this book.
Another factor to consider when buying the batting is its material. Cotton batting is easily washable by hand (check to make sure that it is machine washable), but requires more quilting to keep it in place. Polyester batting of a medium weight is recommended; it doesn't need the extra quilting and is also machine washable.

Bias —
Bias cuts are those that are not parallel to the lengthwise or crosswise grain of the fabric, and should not be made except for special purposes, as the fabric will stretch and distort easily.

Binding —
Is the strip used to cover the raw edges of the quilt to give it a neat appearance, and the name for this covering process. Choice of binding method and material should be planned, not an afterthought, as it contributes to the overall design of the quilt.

Border —
Strips of plain or pieced fabric that are used to frame the entire quilt top. Strips used to frame each individual quilt block are called sashing—see below.

Frame —
A mechanical device used to stretch and hold the fabric while it is being quilted. The frame may be large enough to hold the entire quilt or smaller, such as a hoop that is more portable, and allows working on a small portion of the quilt at any given time.

Grain —
This refers to the fabric's thread directions. Lengthwise grain refers to threads that run parallel to the fabric selvages, while crosswise grain runs from selvage to selvage. Most patterns are meant to run with the grain.

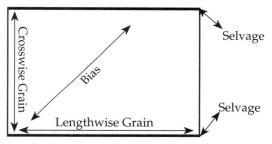

Loft —
This refers to the thickness of the batting material. Batting material usually comes in low, medium, and high loft varieties. See "Batting" above for an explanation of choices.

Mitered corner —
Refers to the method of finishing a quilt border whereby the corners meet at a 45° angle.

Piecing —
The actual sewing of the cut pieces together to form a block, and then the sewing of the blocks together to form the quilt top.

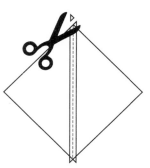

Note:
Make sure that when any two triangles are sewn together, the four tips are cut off each set before proceeding.

Quilt Block —

A section of the quilt top stitched in a regular shape to form a unique unit of the quilt. The shape is usually a geometric one such as a square, rectangle, hexagon, or diamond. These individual units are then sewn together to make the quilt top.

The square, diamond, and hexagon above are three block shapes from patterns included in this book.

Quilt top —

The pieced or appliquéd, decorative part of the quilt that is used as the top layer of the finished quilt.

Quilting —

Can refer to the whole process of making a quilt, or to the specific sewing of the three quilt layers together. This sewing of the layers together holds the batting in place, holds all the layers together, and provides texture and decoration.

Running stitch —

A simple stitch consisting of a series of straight stitches equally spaced, with the stitch length equal to the space between stitches.

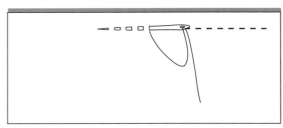

Sashing —

Strips of fabric sewn to the individual quilt blocks to frame them and to isolate each block's design. Many quilts don't use sashing, and allow secondary patterns to form when the individual blocks are sewn together.

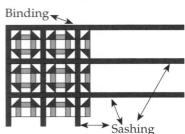 Monkey Wrench without sashing.

Selvage —

The tightly woven fabric edges that run the length of the material on both sides. This selvage needs to be trimmed off and discarded before the quilt pieces are cut out.

Straight grain —

The lengthwise and crosswise grain of the fabric. The two should be perpendicular to each other to be true. If they are not, pull on the fabric at the diagonal corners that are opposite to the direction in which the grain is off. This is important to do before any pieces are cut from the material, as the pieces normally need to be cut with the grain. Pieces cut with the lengthwise grain are much less likely to stretch and distort. Crosswise grain will distort to a small extent, and bias cut pieces are quite easy to stretch and distort.

Template —

The pattern used to mark the fabric for cutting. It is normally made from plastic sheets or a stiff cardboard. Cardboard templates are accurate for only a few markings before their edges are no longer true. Plastic sheet material lasts for many markings and has the advantage of being transparent. Its transparency is a great aid when cutting out patterned pieces that must be cut to the pattern, not with the grain. Make sure all templates are cut out accurately.

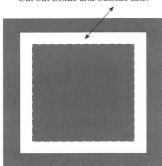

Window template (see page 7)
Cut out inside and outside line.

Quilting Supplies and Equipment

If you are an experienced quilter, you should have all or most of the items listed below. If you are just beginning to quilt, you still may have many of the items. For those supplies that you must purchase, follow the tried and true advice—buy good quality. The small extra expense will pay off with: materials that will last, ease of use, a better finished quilt, and a lot of frustration avoided.

Batting —

Batting is used in sheets as the middle layer of the quilt. It gives the quilt its bulk, texture, and warmth. The batting material is usually 100% cotton, polyester, or a cotton-polyester blend. 100% cotton is washable by hand (check to make sure that it is machine washable), but an extra amount of quilting must be employed in order to keep the batting in place. Since cotton-polyester blend is somewhat of a compromise, we recommend bonded polyester. Bonded polyester batting sheets are also machine washable, but have the advantage that not nearly as much quilting must be done in order to secure the batting to the other two layers of the quilt without slippage.

Batting comes in low, medium, or high-loft varieties. The low-loft requires more quilting (about every 1") to keep it in place. The high-loft is too difficult to quilt through, and is usually tied, not quilted. We recommend the medium-loft batting sheets, as they are easier to quilt through and require less quilting. So with the medium-loft bonded polyester batting you will be able to do as little or as much quilting as you desire, and to do it easily without worrying about slippage.

Beeswax —
This is not essential, but some quilters like to run their thread over beeswax in order to reduce tangling of the thread, and to make the thread go through the three quilt layers more easily.

Clear plastic sheets —
This material can be purchased at most quilt or art supply stores, and is used as a template material. The advantages of using the plastic sheets are that it will continue to make accurate markings on fabric after many uses, and, since it is transparent, lining up a pattern with the template is much easier. This is important when lining up with the fabric pattern is more important than lining up with the grain.

Cutting mat —
This piece of equipment is only necessary if you plan on using a rotary cutter, and is a rough mat used as protection for your table while cutting fabric. It is optional, and frankly, I have never owned one. It can come in handy if you plan on doing a lot of strip piecing.

Iron —
Its use is obvious—pressing fabric before cutting out the pieces and pressing the seam allowances. Use a steam iron, if you have it. If not, use a regular iron with a damp cloth. Do not distort the material while ironing it by moving the iron back and forth. Place the iron down on the fabric, pick it up, and then move it to another spot.

Lightweight cardboard —
Material such as poster board or manila folders that are used for making templates. This works well if the template will only be used moderately, but if sustained use is expected, use clear plastic sheets for the template material.

Marking tools —
These are used to trace the pattern on the fabric before cutting the quilt pieces. They are also used to mark the quilting lines on the quilt top or placement marks for appliqués. There are now special fabric marking pens on the market. These pens will either create a line that will disappear by itself over time, or will wash off with cold water without bleeding. It is certainly a good idea to test these markers on scrap fabric before risking them on a large project such as a quilt (some work well; some are marginal, at best).

A regular #2 pencil, silver-colored pencils, and white fabric marking pencils are also in widespread use. If you use any of them, make sure to keep the point sharp when marking fabric—a dull point adds width to the marked lines, making it difficult to cut the pieces accurately. Use the #2 pencil on light-colored fabric, and the silver- or white-colored fabric marking pencils on dark fabric. Also, if you make a mistake with the pencils, the lines can usually be removed with a soft, white eraser or white art eraser. Do not use an ordinary colored eraser; it will discolor the fabric.

Needle threader —
This device helps to thread needles with small eyes and is optional.

Permanent fine point marker —
This marker is used to trace templates on clear plastic sheets. As with all markers, test to make sure that it will not rub off or bleed on the fabric before using it for any major project such as a quilt.

Quilt soap —
This is a very mild soap used to wash fabric before it is cut and pieced. It will remove the finishes and chemicals which are in the fabric, and that will shorten the quilt's life. A very mild detergent or laundry soap can be used instead, if necessary. Do use one or the other. Simply wetting the fabric will not remove the chemicals that will shorten the fabric's life.

Quilting hoop —
A device made like an embroidery hoop, but much sturdier, so that it can hold the three layers of a quilt firmly together. The normal size for the hoop is 14" to 18", and should not be over 18". Too large a hoop size will make it difficult to sew with one hand under all the quilt layers. The quilting hoop has the advantage over the large quilting frames, as it will allow the project to be portable.

Quilting needles —
These needles are the "betweens," and the recommended sizes for quilting are 8, 9, 10, and 12. These needles are shorter and thinner than regular sewing needles (the higher the number, the shorter the needle). Since they easily allow for short stitches through all three layers of the quilt, they are ideal for quilting. A beginning quilter should start with an 8 or 9 needle, and as your skill level improves, move up to a size 10 or 12.

Quilting thread —
This is a 100% cotton or cotton-covered polyester thread that is stronger than regular sewing thread. It is coated to help penetrate the three quilting layers, and is treated so it will not knot or tangle as easily as regular thread. Traditionally, white is the standard color for quilting thread, but now the thread comes in various colors. It is still a good idea for a beginning quilter to use white or a neutral color, and to then advance to the more colorful threads as your skill level and fine stitching improves.

Rotary cutter —
A device with a round cutting blade mounted on a handle. It is used to cut fabric that is laid against a cutting mat. The rotary cutter is very useful for cut-

ting fabric strips quickly and consistently along the edges of a marked ruler.

Ruler —
Almost any standard ruler is useable, but an 18" or longer plastic ruler with at least 1/8" ruled markings is preferred.

Scissors —
Two pair of scissors are needed—a standard pair for cutting out templates, and a high quality, especially sharp pair for cutting the fabric. Never use the fabric-cutting pair to cut anything else; they will dull easily and produce inaccurate and possibly frayed cut pieces.

Straight pins —
Use long, rustproof pins with large heads. Some quilters use flathead pins for machine quilting. Whichever you use, make sure they are sharp enough to pass easily through the quilt's three layers of material.

Sewing machine —
May be used for all the projects in this book, but the projects were really designed for traditional hand piecing and quilting. If you do machine sew these projects, use a size 12/80 needle.

Sewing needles —
For making the quilt top, use "sharps." These needles are thinner than regular sewing needles and are used for basting, hand piecing, and appliqueing. Use #8 to #12 needles; 9 and 10 being the most popular sizes.

Sewing thread —
A 100% cotton or cotton covered polyester thread used for basting and sewing the quilt pieces together. Do not use your quilting thread for this purpose; it is too heavy and will create too much bulk, especially where seams cross. To prevent show-through, use a neutral color, or a color that blends with the fabric.

Thimble —
This is a necessary item when quilting in order to protect the finger when pushing the needle through three layers of fabric.

Tracing paper —
Any standard grade of tracing paper will work. It is used to trace the quilt pattern so that it can then be transferred to the cardboard template material with transfer paper.

Transfer paper —
Paper for transferring the traced pattern to the cardboard template material. Use a good quality transfer paper, not standard carbon paper, as the carbon is normally too messy and rubs off.

Fabric

Out of necessity our forebears used fabric scraps in order to make their patchwork quilts. I am, personally, a strong proponent for continuing this time-honored practice. This is certainly going against the "contemporary wisdom" of buying fabric especially for each patchwork project, but I feel that much can be said for the charm that the scrap quilts offer. Even though the

fabric requirements are given for each of the traditional quilts presented in this book, I strongly recommend that the wonderful character of the scrap quilt not be abandoned

Without tradition, art is a flock of sheep without a shepherd. Without innovation, it is a corpse.
—WINSTON CHURCHILL

There are, of course, some basic points that should be kept in mind when choosing any fabric for quilting. Try to use the same type fabric throughout any one project—this means that the fabric should be of about the same weight and all washable or non-washable. It makes no practical sense to have the majority of a quilt in a washable material and then use one or two patches that must be dry-cleaned.

The best material for a quilt is 100% cotton, but a cotton blend with a high cotton content can be used. Use one or the other! Do not mix the two if you can avoid it. The cotton material should be smooth, closely woven, light to medium weight, and opaque. 100% cotton will fray less, normally holds its shape better, and is easier to quilt through than cotton blends.

Avoid heavy or stiff fabrics. They make it more difficult to sew the patches and to do the final quilting. Also, the true beauty of the quilt pattern will not show up, because it is almost impossible to get the contours in stiff fabric pronounced enough. Quilting in light fabrics can also cause problems, because the material can be too thin and loosely woven.

For special projects, almost any material can be used, which does not mean that due care should not be exercised. Silks and satins give a rich texture, but are more difficult to work with than 100% cotton. None of the designs in this traditional collection call for it, but materials such as fur and leather have been effectively incorporated into quilts. You should free your imagination and experiment, but let your good taste and common sense be your guide.

Now that I have opened the door a little, I will quickly close it again. In my opinion, always use 100% cotton for any of the quilt projects in this book.

Note: Most manufactures have two new lines of fabric per year and most are not reprints. Since any cloth shop might carry only one bolt of a particular color or pattern, and might not be able to reorder because of a manufacturer's unwillingness to reprint, it is prudent to buy all the material of a certain design at the beginning of the project. For this reason I have been generous in the estimate of fabric needed for any of the quilts in this book.

It is important when you buy any fabric to make sure that the grain is correct. The lengthwise grain should be parallel to the selvage and the cross grain should be at right angles to the selvage. If the grain is not oriented properly, your pieces could become distorted. Always check this before buying fabric of any type.

Fabric Preparation

When any new fabric is purchased, it is necessary to wash and iron it, as well as to remove the selvages. The washing of the fabric as a first step is of extreme importance, and should not be neglected even if you plan on having the finished quilt dry-cleaned. The initial washing process removes the sizing, pre-shrinks the fabric, and makes sure the dyes are colorfast. The material will also be easier to handle (not as slick), easier to quilt through the several layers, and chemicals that may shorten the lifetime of the quilt will be removed. Also, we all know that accidents do happen, and a colorfast fabric will prevent any bleeding of the dyes, in case the quilt becomes wet inadvertently. Some of the heavier dyes can also simply rub off during normal usage.

Black and the dark primary colors (red, green, and blue) are especially prone to bleed when washed. To check this, agitate part of the material in warm water and wring the moisture out. If any of the color bled, make sure to wash that fabric by itself. It may be necessary to wash a heavily dyed fabric four or five times to eliminate all of the bleeding. If you can see the rinse water, wash until the water runs clear. If you can't see the rinse water, add a small piece of white fabric to the wash and check it to see if the colored fabric lost any dye.

Tips:

1. Use soap made for fine fabrics or a very mild detergent.

2. Before washing, cut the four corners of the fabric diagonally at a 45° angle to prevent raveling of the fabric.

3. It is possible to help hold the colorfastness of the fabric by adding a cupful of vinegar to the rinse water.

4. Do not use a fabric softener since this will prevent the removal of all the sizing.

5. Rinse two or three times to remove all the finishing chemicals.

6. It is quite important that all the fabrics for the quilt are washed. If some are and some aren't, the quilt may show signs of stretching or puckering in places when the whole quilt is finally washed.

All of this washing and rinsing may sound excessive, but if you think about it for a minute, you will realize that it isn't. The quilt you will make from the fabric is a tangible representation of yourself. This is reason enough to be thorough. Also, making the quilt will take a considerable amount of your time, and to skimp on this important step is not prudent. By following the washing procedure, you will be able to pass on a beautiful quilt to your children and your children's children.

Color and Patterns

Since it can be the first thing that is noticed when we see a finished quilt, color is of great importance. This should be looked on as an excellent opportunity to express yourself and to enhance the overall effect of the visual impact of your quilt. Unfortunately, color is such a subjective matter that it is impossible to present any hard and fast rules that everyone might agree to. The best that can be done is to offer some general guidelines. I have done so below, and I hope they will be of help in your decision making.

1. Try to be consistent in your choice of colors as to the overall effect that you wish to convey.

Normally use bright colors with bright colors and subdued colors with other subdued colors, since mixing the two sends contradictory signals to the viewer.

2. The tones used in the quilt are usually the most important consideration in making the design of the individual blocks stand out — as opposed to the color itself, which is more noticeable in the impact of the quilt as a whole. Therefore, make the contrast of the colors distinct to give a sense of a bold block design. Use a dark tone with a light tone, or a light tone with a medium or dark tone. If you want the block design to be dominant, avoid using colors of the same tone next to each other (medium next to medium, dark next to dark, etc.). Only when you want to subordinate the block design and to emphasize the total quilt design would you use similar tones next to each other when piecing the block. See page 12 for additional information.

3. Prints are a very useful tool in the design of your project. In fact, many quilts are done using only printed fabric. This can be done quite effectively, if the tones of the printed fabric give good piece separation and the printed pattern does not overpower. I find that it is better to use a small to medium pattern which contains at least two of the dominant colors of the quilt. Large patterns are more difficult to use, and I, personally, have never liked the look of large patterns being broken up to accommodate small block pieces — I like at least one complete representation of the pattern to show in each piece.

It is also worth noting that the use of very strong directional patterns such as stripes or plaids is much more difficult to handle well. If you do decide on a directional pattern, be sure to cut the block pieces using the direction of the pattern as a guide, and not the grain of the fabric, unless the two happen to coincide.

This will mean that at times the fabric will be cut on the bias and will not be as stable. This point is worth considering, but should not discourage you from the use of directional patterns that will add the desired touch to your quilt.

4. It might be surprising, but the amount of quilting that you plan on doing to finish the quilt has an impact on the colors and patterns you use. It is obvious that solid-colored fabrics will show the final quilting pattern more prominently than a patterned fabric. It is then common sense to choose distinct patterns (especially a small pattern) to help negate the fact that the finished piece will not be heavily quilted. Conversely, in order to show off intricate and lavish quilting patterns, it is wise to use solids. This is especially true if the quilting is to be done in a contrasting color of thread.

5. If your quilt will have a border, it is best to tie the design together by choosing one or more of the quilt's main colors for the border also. Another approach is to use a color that has a striking contrast to the main quilt colors. Do one or the other! Don't leave any doubt about your intentions in the minds of viewers by trying a compromise.

Finally, if the quilt is for your own use — suit yourself. Choose colors to match the decor of the room that it will be displayed in, or to express a mood, to incorporate some fabric that you have on hand, or any of a thousand other reasons that strike your fancy. Quiltmaking should be an enjoyable pastime, not a burden, and who's to say that your taste isn't as good as anyone else's.

I agree with no man's opinion.
I have some of my own.
—IVAN TURGENEV

Pressing

Carefully pressing the sewn pieces may seem like a mundane task, but it is of vital importance for a well-made quilt. Not only is the finished quilt's appearance enhanced, but you will find that in many cases pressing will actually save time and definitely save frustration. If the pieces are not pressed, there is no practical way to get the individual pieces or the unit blocks to fit together properly.

It is necessary, in machine piecing, to press as you go. With hand piecing, you usually wait until a unit block is completed before pressing. It is normal practice to press the two seam allowances in the same direction to give added strength to the seam, and to press toward the darker fabric in order to minimize show-through on the right side of the quilt top.

These are guidelines that should be followed on most pieced quilts, but in some situations you may have to press a seam open or in the direction of the lighter fabric in order to reduce bulk. You may need to press the seams open, for example, when all the sewn pieces meet at a center point. Also, in sewing rows together, the seams need to be in opposite directions, not only to reduce bulk at any overlap, but to make the seams line up properly. Press the seam allowances first, and then turn the fabric pieces over and press the right side. Use the pressing technique described earlier—picking the iron up and placing it back down on the fabric instead of using a sliding motion.

Making Templates and Cutting Pieces

Making accurate templates and cutting precise fabric pieces is of vital importance to any quilt project. The key word here is consistency. Each of us will trace the templates, cut them out, and mark and cut the fabric slightly differently. This is to be expected, and should cause you little concern. If your pieces come out slightly larger or smaller than the drawn patterns in this book, it will simply mean that each pieced block will be a little larger or smaller than the indicated 12 inches, and consequently, so will the overall dimensions of the quilt. The prime factor is that the individual blocks you make be of the same size so they will join together correctly to make the finished quilt. If you are consistent in marking and cutting each piece the same way, this will happen automatically.

This is not to imply that when making the template you should not make it as closely as possible to the drawn pattern. The closer you are, the better you can plan for a precise overall finished quilt size—if this is a primary consideration. Also, if the cut pieces vary from the pattern by too great a margin, the individual blocks will be difficult to sew together. Always check the finished template by placing if over the drawn patterns in the book to see that they are the same size at the center of the drawn lines. As mentioned above, a slight variation is to be expected, but it is important that the deviation be minimal. Take care in the work you do—but don't be obsessive.

A good beginning
makes a good ending.
—ENGLISH PROVERB

If you use clear plastic sheets (a good idea) that are available in most craft or art supply stores, trace over the outline of the pattern with a fine point, permanent marker. Include the outline, letter designation, arrow to indicate the grain line, and quite importantly, the name of the quilt you are making.

If you are using cardboard for the template material (which is accurate for only a few tracings), trace the outline of the pattern onto thin tracing paper. Trace this onto the cardboard using any standard transfer paper with the dark side toward the cardboard. Include the letter designation, arrow, etc. as with the plastic templates.

All of the patterns in this book include a 1/4" seam allowance. Many quilt publications suggest that you trace only the dark outside cutting line for pieces that will be machine sewn. This is due to the fact that many sewing machines have a 1/4" distance between the outer edge of the presser foot and the needle, and will give you the 1/4" seam allowance automatically as you sew. If this setting for your machine is different and cannot be adjusted, it is a simple matter to place guide tape (masking tape strips) on the sewing machine platform at the proper distance from the needle.

These same publications suggest that for hand sewing, trace only the dotted line of the pattern for the finished piece size. If this is done, then an extra 1/4" space is approximated around the entire template for the seam allowance when tracing it to the fabric. With this method the traced line on the fabric is the seam line on which to sew.

I suggest that you use the dark outside line of the pattern for the template no matter which sewing method you use. By doing so, the cut fabric pieces will all be of consistent sizes, will enable you to machine or hand sew the blocks (important if others do some of the blocks), and will usually enable you to get the most pieces from a given fabric. If this technique is used, then the 1/4" seam allowance is marked on the fabric piece with a ruler just before the pieces are sewn together.

One other technique is to make a window template. Do this by marking and cutting along both the solid outline and the dotted line. This produces a template with the center section cut out. It is then a simple matter to mark the fabric cutting line using the outside of the template and to very quickly mark the seam allowance at the same time by tracing around the inside of the template.

Use whatever method best suits your own needs when drawing the templates. Then cut them out with scissors (not the scissors used for fabric cutting, as the fabric scissors must remain absolutely sharp to give clean cuts of the material with minimum fraying). A single-edged razor-blade or a craft knife such as an X-Acto can also be used—be quite careful not to apply too much pressure and break the blade.

After the template(s) are made, place them down on the wrong side of the fabric and trace them with a fabric marking pen. It is important to test the pen on a small piece of fabric to make sure the marking will not show through to the other side, and that it will not bleed when washed. Some specially-made pens will make a mark that will disappear over a short period of time. Others will disappear with the application of cold water without bleeding. Again—do make sure you test any marking pen on a small piece of scrap fabric by

marking and washing the fabric before starting your main quilt project.

It is very important to double-check the accuracy of your templates before you cut all the fabric for your project. Do this by marking and cutting only enough pieces of fabric for one sample block. After the sample block is pieced and checked to see that the pieces fit properly, continue to mark and cut out the fabric for the entire quilt.

Note: Be aware that the true dimensions of the patterns lie on the center of each drawn line, not on the inside or outside of the line. Draw your template accordingly and cut it out as close to the center of the line as possible. When the template is traced to the wrong side of the fabric, it will be too big by the thickness of the drawn line, so use a sharp marking pen and cut the fabric out toward the inside of the line.

Piecing the Block

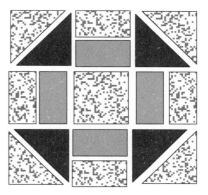

A good idea, especially for beginning quilters, is to lay out all the pieces needed for a block in their exact position before you actually start sewing the pieces together. After this is done, follow the step-by-step instructions provided for each quilt to piece the block. Put the first two pieces of fabric together with the right sides facing each other. Make sure your sewing line is visible and the seam allowance is at least 1/4". It is very important to sew a straight running stitch and to maintain the exact finished size of the piece when sewing each set. If you are off 1/16" on each set of pieces, by the time you have set the entire block and then set the blocks together, you are off by a quite noticeable amount. The important thing is consistency of the finished size of the sewn pieces. Since the seams will not show, it is quite okay and usually necessary to make small adjustments in the seam allowance in order to get the finished pieces to be exact. Keep this in mind—a sewn 2" square needs to be exactly 2" whether the seam allowance is 3/16", 1/4", 5/16", etc. The projects in this book are intended for hand piecing, but may be done by machine. Since traditional hand quilting is stressed, only the basic set up for machine quilting is given below. Only an experienced user of a sewing machine should machine piece, as such situations as sewing into corners and sewing diamonds or hexagons are a lot easier done by hand.

If you machine piece, use a straight stitch and about 10 to 14 stitches per inch with a size 12/80 needle. Many sewing machines have the outer edge of the presser foot 1/4″ from the placement of the needle, giving the standard 1/4″ seam allowance automatically. If your machine doesn't, and is not adjustable, place strips of masking tape 1/4″ from the needle hole to act as a guide.

Note: In order not to damage the needle or jam the machine, make sure all pins are removed from the fabric before reaching the machine's sewing position.

For hand quilting, follow the general guidelines at the beginning of this section. Use a small running stitch with a single 18″ length of 100% cotton or cotton covered polyester sewing (not quilting) thread. Make sure to stay within the boundaries of the marked sewing lines— do not sew into the seam allowance when hand piecing. Begin and end each seam with backstitching to secure the thread.

The key words in piecing are consistency and accuracy. Make sure the finished piece that shows on the right side of the quilt is the right size, even if this means slight adjustments to the seam allowance. Also make sure the stitches are small and evenly placed.

Always mark, cut and piece a sample block before marking and cutting out all the fabric for the quilt.

Borders

A border may or may not be added to a quilt at the discretion of the maker. It is important to understand that the border will have a significant visual impact on the overall presentation of the quilt and it should, therefore, be planned for, not added as an afterthought. The border will serve as a frame for the inner patchwork, but it is sometimes used to bring the finished dimensions of a quilt to a specific size. If the border is used just for sizing the quilt, it is still of no less importance to have a definite plan for its execution—it will have an impact.

Since there are so many variables in the piecing of a quilt, such as the characteristics of the fabric, bias or non-bias cuts, exact seam allowance used, etc., it is not prudent to judge the finished size of the quilt until the inner patchwork is completed. After this is done, measure the quilt on all sides to ascertain the actual quilt dimensions—this is important because it is likely that the opposite sides will not be equal.

It is normal procedure to cut single fabric borders in one piece along the lengthwise grain of the fabric. This means that for a 108″ quilt you would have to buy 3 yards of fabric, plus an extra 4-6″ for shrinkage and 1/2″ for a seam allowance, or about 3 1/4 yards. Another method is to piece the fabric to make the final length. If this is done, make only one seam and place it

at the center of the pieced strip. Also, cut the ends of the strips that will be joined on the bias at 45°, not straight across, as this will be less noticeable. With this method, only about 1 3/4 yards of material will be needed. Even less material will be needed if the strips are cut on the crosswise grain, and this can be done for smaller quilts if desired. But any quilt with a dimension of about 90″ or above will need at least three pieces sewn together to give sufficient length, and this is not recommended.

Another popular border treatment is to make a pieced border that accentuates or dramatically contrasts the patchwork pattern of the inner quilt. Pieced squares, rectangles, triangles, diamonds, or other geometric shapes are used in the same manner as for the main patchwork. This is very effective, and there are no extra quilting procedures that you need to know in order to make beautiful pieced borders.

It is a bad plan that admits of no modification.
—PUBLILIUS SYRUS

There are, however, two cautionary notes. First be sure that the scale of the design that you will use for the border is evenly divisible into the dimensions of the inner quilt. For example, if the patchwork piece is 3″ in depth, make sure the quilt dimension for the depth of the inner quilt is evenly divisible by 3 (or whatever the piece depth may be). The same is true for the width, of course—if the width is 2″, then it is necessary that the width of the inner quilt can be evenly divided by 2. If this is not the case, you can reconcile the different sizes in a couple of ways. One, you can rescale the border pieces to fit the dimensions of the quilt, or you can add a plain border between the inner quilt and the pieced border that will bring the quilt size up to one that is evenly divisible by the pattern that you currently have. The second potential problem is with the corners. It is a wise decision to plan them carefully, either making a small sketch or actually piecing a corner section with a small section of border strip to see that they will work together. One easy solution is to make the corners from a solid piece of fabric. This forms blunt corners on the quilt, and is recommended for most quilts. A mitered corner is readily visible only with borders that show a strong directional pattern such as striped material. Since this type of corner is more difficult and time consuming to do, it is used only for these special cases.

After the border strips are cut or pieced, attach them to the quilt with a 1/4″ seam allowance and the same running stitch that you used when piecing the quilt. If the border was pieced with a variation of the inner patchwork and is to scale, it will be necessary to give the border extra care in order to make sure the seams meet properly. Sew the lengthwise border strips on first. Do this after the measurement of both of the long sides of the quilt has been made. Cut the borders to fit the shorter side if there is a difference—if this difference is too great, it will entail adjusting the seam allowance on some of the block pieces. If the sides are only slightly different in size, sew the border to the shorter side first after marking the midpoint and quarter points of both the strip and the inner quilt and matching up these points. Now proceed with the side of the quilt that is slightly longer. Again, match the marked center point and quarter points of the strip and the quilt. Pin the two together at these points, and then ease out any fullness of the quilt evenly as you sew. Repeat the same procedure as above for the width of the quilt, starting with the shorter side (if any). **Note:** It will be quite obvious after the two side strips are sewn on, that when taking the measurements for the widths, the side strips must be included. This may be overlooked if the measurements are taken before the side strips are sewn—it has happened.

Note: A common practice is to use the same material for both the quilt top and the border(s). If you plan on doing so, make sure to cut the border strips before you cut out any of the patchwork pieces to ensure that you will have enough long fabric for the borders.

Marking the Quilt Top

Before the actual quilting can take place, any quilting design must be drawn on the quilt top. This is not necessary for quilting "in the ditch" (quilting very close to the seam or appliqué), and if one is very careful, marking may not be necessary for "outline" quilting (quilting approximately 1/4" from the seam or appliqué). If you feel that marking the outline is necessary, doing so before the quilt layers are basted together will usually be the easiest. For "ornamental" quilting (more elaborate designs or repeating patterns), it is always necessary to draw the pattern before quilting. **Note:** A variation of "outline" quilting called "echo" quilting is also used and is simply repeats of the outline at 1/4" intervals outward from the seam or appliqué.

Mark the design(s) on the right side of the quilt top after placing it on a hard, flat surface. It might be necessary to place the quilt top on the floor for convenience if it is quite large. Some quilters prefer to wait until the quilt layers are basted together and mounted in a frame or hoop before marking small portions of the design at a time. This method works well for less intricate designs, but it is normally better to mark more complicated patterns on the flat quilt top before the quilt layers are put together. If the design is marked before layering, make sure to use one of the more durable marking methods, as it needs to last through all the rest of the quilting process.

Simple, straight-line patterns such as horizontal, vertical, or diagonal designs can be easily placed on the quilt top with a taut chalk line such as a carpenter or mason might use. The end points must be precisely marked for this method, but it is quick and gives perfectly straight lines. After making the initial chalk lines, go over them with a more permanent marker if you know the subsequent quilting will require excessive handling—if the quilt is mounted in a large frame this probably will not be necessary.

Needle marking can be used for small areas at a time, such as those encountered in quilting in a hoop. A large blunt needle is used very much as one would use a pencil to make a visible and, of course, temporary indentation on the quilt top. A ruler or yardstick can be used for marking straight lines, while a template or stencil is used as a guide for more elaborate designs.

For the most intricate quilting designs, use perforated patterns. Place the patterns on the quilt top and use pounce (a fine powder) to rub over the perforations. This powder design is usually enough for small areas for hoop quilting. Otherwise, trace over the transferred powder design with a more permanent marker. Perforated patterns can be made by tracing the design on paper and then making the perforations with a sharp pin or by sewing over the tracing with an unthreaded sewing machine.

For those designs in between the simple and intricate, use a template very similar in principle to the ones used to mark the fabric pieces for the patchwork top. The templates are made from cardboard in the same manner as the templates for the fabric pieces. If the template is for a repeating design that overlaps, it is convenient to place a notch or mark on the template to indicate the point of overlap, making it easy to line up the template.

As for the actual marking, use a hard lead pencil with a sharp point, chalk, or a marking pen. Sometimes the lines made with the hard lead pencil will not readily come out. It is recommended only for designs that will be completely covered with special stitching, such as chain stitches. The chalk is fine if the quilting will not entail a great deal of additional handling—such as small areas quilted in a hoop or even a whole quilt if the quilt layers are already mounted in a large frame and not rolled up. The needle-marking method can also be used for this purpose if you wish to work on small areas at a time.

For more permanent markings, use a special marking pen that has ink that is easily removed with cold water. There are also marking pens that will produce lines that fade in a few hours that are useful for marking small areas at a time. When using a permanent marking pen, always test scrap fabric to make sure all the ink can be removed, and that there is no bleeding on the fabric before you mark a completed quilt top.

Attaching Batting and Backing

The final quilt is composed of three layers: top, batting, and backing. The piecing of the top has already been discussed, and a detailed explanation of batting materials was given in the sections: "Quilting Terms" and

"Quilting Supplies and Equipment." Normally the backing is made from a single fabric material. If muslin is used for the backing, it comes in 90" widths and usually is wide enough for most quilts without having to piece. Also, other backing fabrics are now coming on the market that are 60", 90", and 108" in width.

If you cannot purchase a wide enough fabric for your quilt, sew three pieces together to make the backing. It is possible to use only two pieces and to place the seam in the center, but this is not recommended—the center is the natural folding place for the quilt and takes a great deal of stress. Cut a center strip 36-44" wide, and add a strip on each side to make the final desired size. It is recommended that you use a 1/2" seam allowance for the backing to also compensate for added stress, and to press the seams open, not to one side.

It is possible to have a more pieced appearance to the quilt backing, employing any fabric scrap that you might have. This idea can be taken to the point where you have, in effect, a reversible quilt with either side being suitable for display. Not an entirely bad idea, as it opens up even more options for your creative urges. For the correct size of the backing and batting, please see the section on binding.

After the backing is made, the three layers must be placed in the correct orientation. Make sure the backing is pressed and facing wrong side up. On top of this, center the batting, and for the final layer, center the quilt top right side up. To help in this centering process, place marks at the center points on all sides of each of the layers. Another method is to fold each layer separately in half and then in half again in the opposite direction. This will form a crease that will meet at the center of each. Use this center point for alignment, placing center point on center point. In this method unfold the backing material flat and wrong side up. With the batting still folded into quarters, place the corner of the batting fold (its center point) on the center of the backing material and simply unfold. Do the quilt top in exactly the same manner.

There are several methods for basting the three layers together before quilting. In each case, start at the center of the quilt and work toward the edges. Normally baste out to within 1/2" of the quilt edges, and then baste around the perimeter of the quilt maintaining the baste line 1/2" from the quilt top's edge. Start this process by using sharp safety pins to hold the layers together. Work from the center out horizontally and then vertically, making a cross through the center of the quilt. Then work from these lines in parallel rows about 4" apart—first horizontally and then vertically. After pinning, baste with large running stitches. If the batting is thick or intricate quilting is to be done, baste the lines about 3-4" apart. If you have medium to thin batting and moderate quilting designs the basting lines can be 4-6" apart.

After basting, remove the safety pins, and the quilt layers are ready to be mounted on a frame or hoop. Or, use the quicker method of pin basting where the safety pins are placed about 3" apart to secure the three layers, and no additional basting is done with needle and thread.

Quilting

The quilting (sewing together of the three quilt layers) can be done on a large frame, a hoop, on the lap, or on any firm, flat surface. A fixed quilting frame is convenient in that the whole quilt is exposed at one time, so several people can work on it at once, but most quilters just don't have the large working area needed to keep a fixed frame in place long enough to finish their project. A frame that allows the quilt to be rolled up with a smaller area exposed is more economical in space, but it is still rather large and somewhat unwieldy. For most people the quilting hoop (see the section on "Supplies and Equipment" for a description) is more preferable.

Regardless of which of these methods you use, always start quilting from the center, working toward the edges. The batting will tend to creep a little as you quilt the layers together, and by starting at the center, you can work the batting toward the quilt's edges, preventing any puckers. If a hoop is used, mount the center of the quilt in the hoop and secure it so that you have a smooth, taut surface (check both sides) to work with. Do not make the layers as taut as you would for embroidery work, as this will make the quilting rather difficult—just a flat, smooth surface is needed.

When quilting, the sewing hand is kept above the quilt to manipulate the needle, while the other hand is placed under the quilt in order to detect when the needle has penetrated all three layers. It is necessary to use a thimble on the middle finger of the sewing hand in order to force the needle through all the layers, and it is advisable to wrap the finger used under the quilt with masking tape to prevent it's being repeatedly stuck.

Quilt with a sharp quilting needle and one strand of quilting thread that is 18-20" long. Don't use thread that is longer than this because it will tangle. Tie a knot at the long end of the thread and insert the needle into just the top layer 1/2-1" from the place you want to start quilting. Bring the needle out at the desired quilting point and give it a sharp, firm tug to pop the knot into the batting layer so that it will be hidden. Now push the needle through all three layers of the quilt. When you feel the needle come through the bottom layer, bring it back up through all three layers. The stitches will all be simple running stitches that are placed 8-10 per inch and evenly spaced on both the top and bottom layer. This spacing is, of course, equal to the amount of needle that is showing before you force it through the quilt in the opposite direction. For the beginning quilter, stitching with 5-7 stitches per inch is expected, but a thoroughly experienced quilter may get 12 per inch. To begin with, try for an even stitch on the quilt top and backing, and the number of stitches per inch will come in due course. When you finish with one length of thread, tie a knot in it and pull it through to the batting as you did the beginning knot. Since the beginning and ending stitches will not appear exactly the same as the running stitches, try to place them at a seam or where the quilting crosses. Naturally, this is not always possible. Doing so is a good idea, but is not mandatory by any means.

> *What we hope ever to do with ease, we must learn first to do with diligence.*
>
> –SAMUEL JOHNSON

After you finish the entire quilt, remove the basting, except for the basting that was placed at the perimeter, 1/2" from the edges. This is left in place for the next step, which is binding the quilt. The basting can also be cut and removed as you are working in order to facilitate the the actual quilting process, but this should be done only in the immediate working area.

Binding

The final step in making a quilt is to apply the binding. There are numerous ways to do this, and the most common methods will be discussed here. I do make the suggestion that if you employ one of the separate binding methods, you cut the material from the lengthwise grain. It has been suggested that a bias strip for binding is more durable; in fact, the same number of threads are present at any given point of the fabric no matter how it is cut. Also, my own personal experience has not indicated any significant advantage to using bias-cut binding strips. Bias-cut material is, however, necessary for binding quilts that have curved edges. All of the quilts in this book have straight edges, and there is no problem using strips cut on the lengthwise grain. If it is necessary to piece strips together, do so using the same method as described for piecing together border strips (i.e. cut ends at 45° angle, place cut edges together with right sides of fabric touching, and sew with a 1/4" seam allowance).

One of the easiest methods of binding is the self-binding method. If the quilt has a border, or the backing fabric is of good quality, this method can be used. If the backing material is the one that will provide the material for the binding, cut the quilt top and batting to the finished quilt size, and cut the backing larger. The extra size the backing must be all around the quilt is equal to the size of the binding you desire plus 1/2" seam allowance plus 1/8" to 1/4" for the thickness of the quilt (e.g. if you want a 3/4" binding, make the backing 3/4" + 1/2" + 1/8" = 1 3/8" wider on all sides). Press under the 1/2" seam allowance, wrap the backing fabric edge around to the top of the quilt, and slip-stitch the binding in place. Of course, if you have a border on the quilt, you can do the reverse—cut the backing and batting to exact finished size, make the border larger by

the desired size plus seam allowance, wrap the border fabric around to the back of the quilt, and slip-stitch in place. Another self-binding method is to cut the batting about 1/4" smaller than the top and backing. Then the top and backing fabric are each turned to the inside of the quilt, and slip-stitched together.

The easiest separate binding method is to use a long binding strip down each side of the quilt. With this method the three layers of the quilt should all be cut to the same size. The strip's width should be equal to 2 times the desired binding width plus 2 times the seam allowance plus 1/8" to 1/4" for the thickness of the quilt (e.g. if you want a 3/4" binding, make the strip 2(3/4) + 2(1/4) + 1/8 = 2 1/8"). After cutting the strips, place the raw edges together lengthwise with the wrong sides touching, and press. Open the strip and place it on one side of the quilt top with the raw edges in alignment lengthwise and the right sides of the fabric together; pin in place. (Place the strips in the same order as you did for the borders.) Sew the binding strip to the quilt, sewing through all four layers (binding strip, top, batting, and backing) using a 1/4" seam allowance. After the first strip is sewn, wrap it around the quilt, turn in the seam allowance and slip-stitch it to the backing material. Sew the opposite side in exactly the same way. After completing the sides, the top and bottom strips are sewn in place. For each of these, cut the binding strip 1" longer than the width of the quilt so that when you align the strip to the quilt 1/2" can be extended on each end of the quilt top. This 1/2" extra length is turned under to the wrong side at each end, thus preventing a raw edge from showing at the quilt corners. With this being done, proceed with the sewing as you did for the other two sides.

A variation of this is called the French fold method. In essence you are doubling the thickness of the fabric that will be used for the binding. The formula for the strip width is 2 times the seam allowance plus 4 times the desired binding width plus 1/8" to 1/4" for the quilt thickness (e.g. if you want a 3/4" binding, make the strip 2(1/4) + 4(3/4) + 1/8" = 3 5/8"). Follow the general instructions given in the paragraph above with the exception that the binding strip is not unfolded after it is pressed lengthwise. Leaving the strip folded double and sewing both layers to the quilt will, of course, double the thickness of the binding. This might help stabilize the quilt a little more and may prevent some tears, but it will not otherwise increase the longevity of the quilt. This is due to the fact that it is just as easy to wear through the outside fabric layer of the French fold as it is to wear through the one layer of standard fold. If either one happens, it is time for a new binding.

> A quilt is a work of art so you might think of signing your name or initials and adding the date as artists sign their work. A strip of muslin may be used on which to embroider this information. Sew the strip to a back corner of the quilt.

11

Tone Combinations and Secondary Patterns

The illustrations on this page and the following five pages are to demonstrate the importance of selecting the proper tone combinations for your quilt. If no sashing is used to separate the individual blocks in the quilt, secondary patterns are often formed when the blocks are sewn together. This does not have to be a problem. In fact, if the quilt fabric tones are chosen with care, this is just another opportunity to place your own personal stamp on the quilt.

The quilt block chosen for the illustrations is for the Bow Tie quilt, but any other could have been used.

It is important in your work to understand this concept. No matter how experienced a quiltmaker is, it is almost impossible to visualize how the final quilt will appear when the blocks are pieced together. That is why those with experience are in the habit of making a sketch that includes at least a four-block section of the quilt. This sketch is used to experiment with different tone values and to see the secondary patterns set up, if any.

This book includes a set of outline illustrations of a four-block combination for every quilt. This is to save your time so that you will not have to make a sketch of the blocks for yourself. Please feel free to photocopy any of these designs that are given in outline form on pages 18-23. This permission is not intended to negate the copyright protection of this book as a whole. Permission to freely reproduce the contents is only granted for pages 18-23.

Do make photocopies and experiment.

Illustrations of the quilts, along with the step-by-step instructions for their piecing, start on page 24. Note that in each case the quilt shown at the upper left corner is the one that is described in the instructions on the subsequent page.

The smaller quilt illustration(s) below or to the right of the top quilt illustration is there to demonstrate the principle of tone selection described above and on the following five pages.

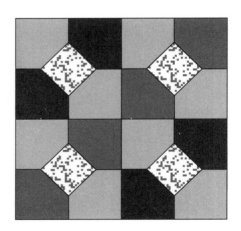

This is the original block as shown in the step-by-step instuctions for this quilt pattern.

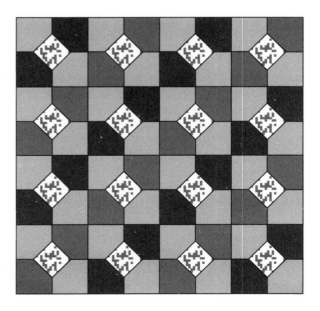

There are no strong secondary patterns set up, and the overall effect is that of interacting, but separate bow ties.

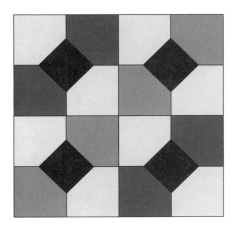

Notice that the bow ties in the upper left and lower right corners don't have enough contrast, as the center knot of the tie and the two adjoining darker pieces are too close in tone to each other.

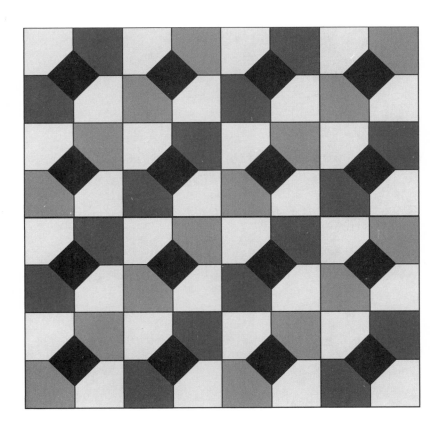

Hold the page at arm's length to see the secondary patterns that are produced from this tone selection.

Three separate, strong patterns are produced. These patterns conflict with each other for attention and are not a good choice.

There is a better separation of tones in this block, with no similar tones next to each other.

Hold the page at arm's length to see the secondary patterns that are produced from this tone selection.

A very strong and pleasing secondary pattern is set up with this tone combination.

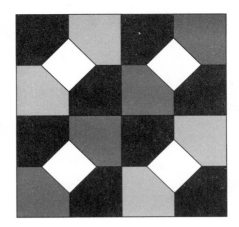

White tones of this block come forward, while the dark tones recede.

Hold the page at arm's length to see the secondary patterns that are produced from this tone selection.

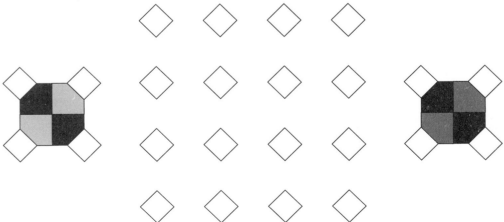

At least three secondary patterns are present, but the overall effect is pleasing, as the separate patterns do not conflict with each other.

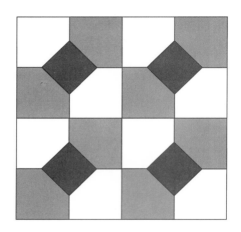

This block has good tone separation with strong diagonal lines.

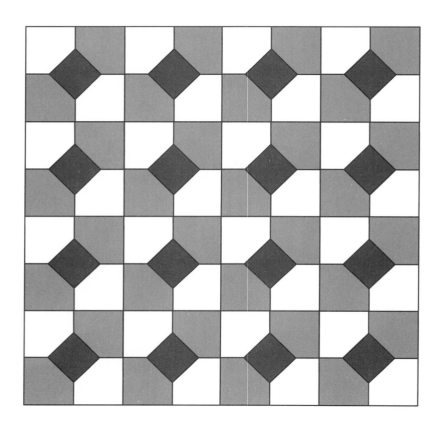

Hold the page at arm's length to see the secondary patterns that are produced from this tone selection.

This tone combination has produced one strong secondary pattern.

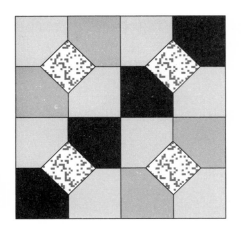

This block has poor tone separation, especially in the upper left and lower right corners.

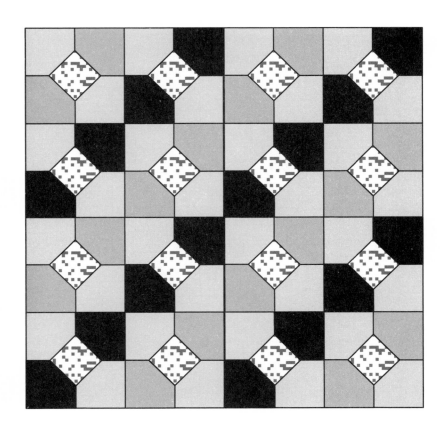

Hold the page at arm's length to see the secondary patterns that are produced from this tone selection.

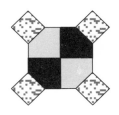

This is the one strong secondary pattern set up by this combination of tones.

Four-Block Outlines

This page and the following five pages contain four-block outlines of all the quilts that are presented in this book. They are here for your convenience in deciding on the tone combinations that you will use in your quilt projects.

The outline below is large enough to use at 100%—just photocopy as many versions as you desire and then fill in the separate squares with different tones combinations until you are satisfied with your results. It is recommended that for the other outlines shown that you have them copied at 200%, which will make them the same size of the outline below.

For a detailed explanation of this process and examples of the results that you can expect, see the previous six pages.

The granting permission for free use of these six pages (18-23) in no way negates the overall copyright of this book—the free use is granted for pages 18-23 only. But do make copies of them and experiment. You will be much more pleased with the finished project and will help in the development of your eye for pleasing tone combinations. It's also a lot of fun—trust me on this.

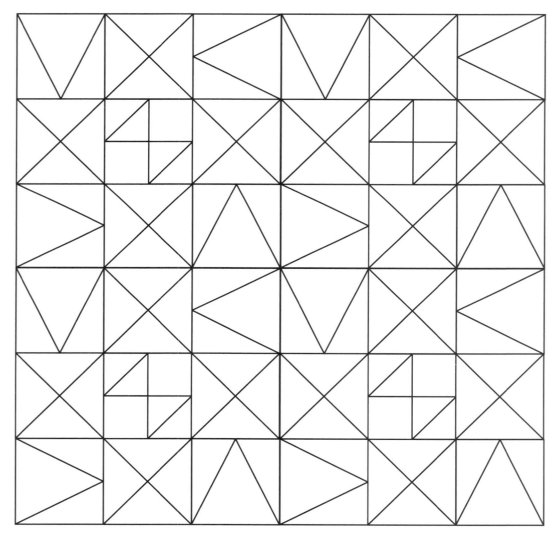

All in a Spin

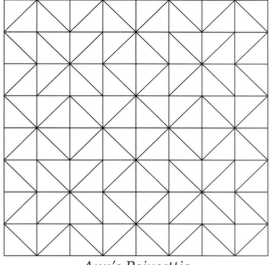

Ann's Poinsettia

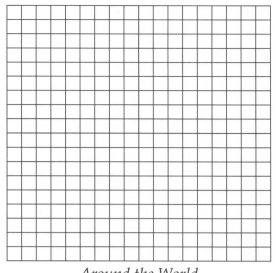

Around the World

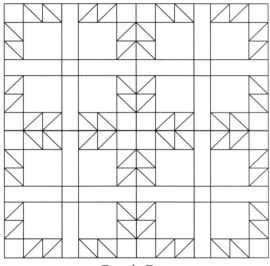

Bear's Paw

Birds in the Air

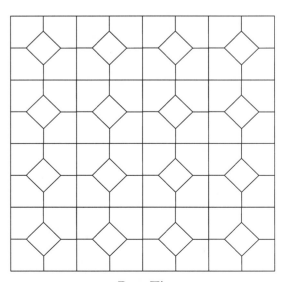

Bow Tie

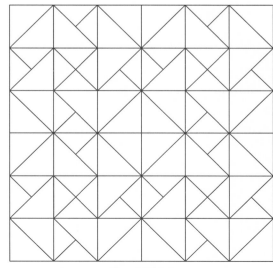

Card Trick

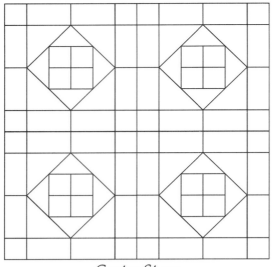

Center Stage

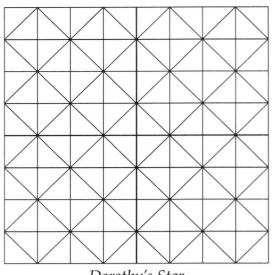

Dorothy's Star

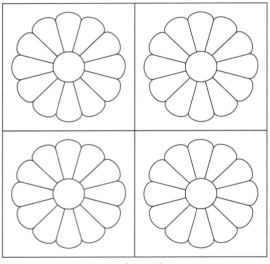

Dresden Plate

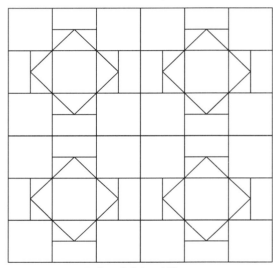

Friendship Album

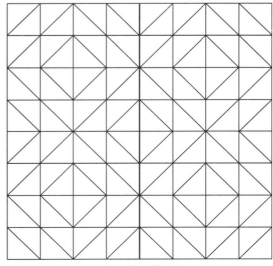

Garden Path

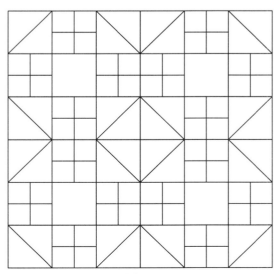

Gold Mine

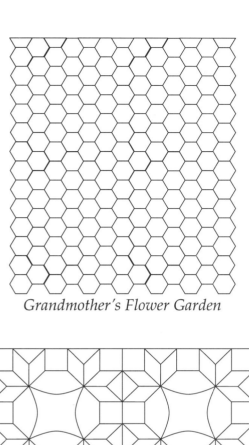

Grandmother's Flower Garden

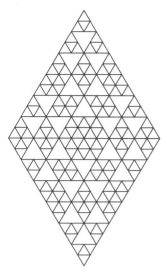

Granny's Diamond

Hands All Around

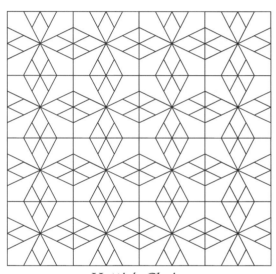

Hattie's Choice

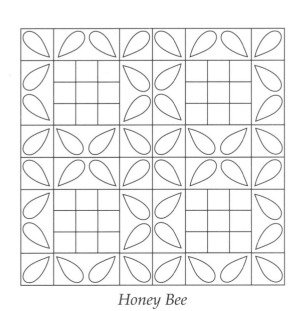

Honey Bee

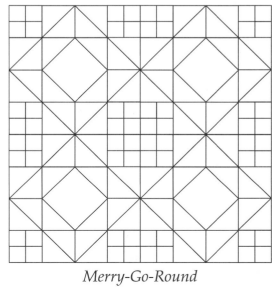

Merry-Go-Round

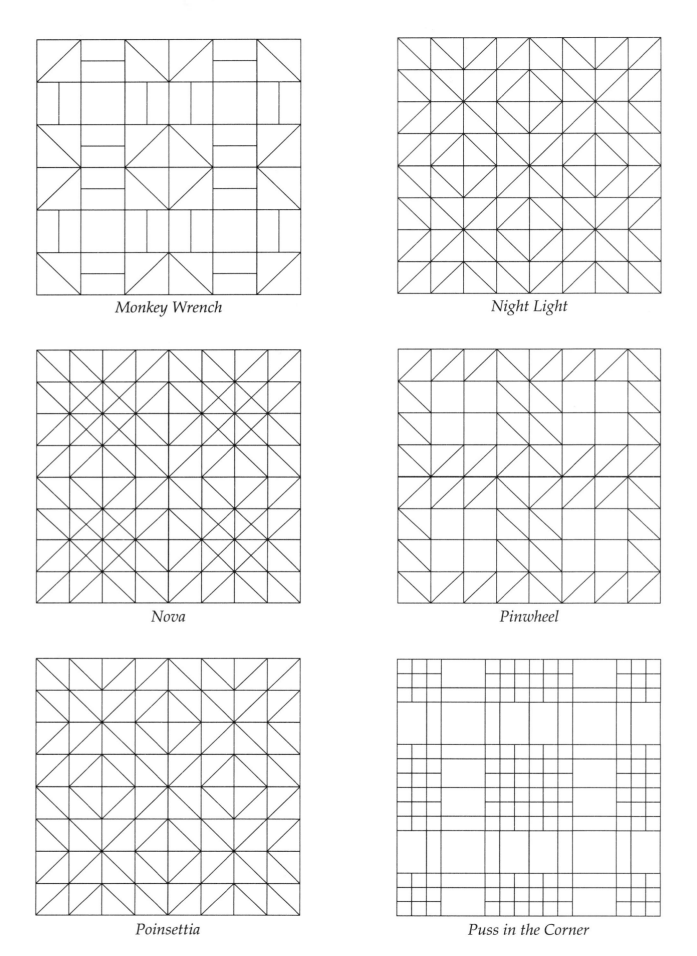

Monkey Wrench

Night Light

Nova

Pinwheel

Poinsettia

Puss in the Corner

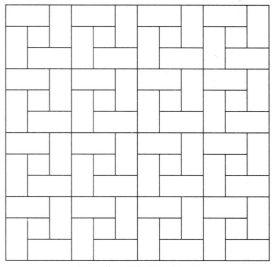

Road with No End

See pages 12–18 for an explanation of the four-block outlines shown on these pages (18–23).

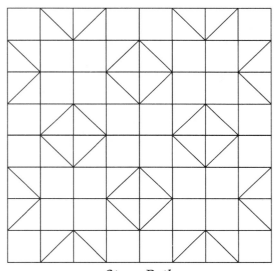

Stone Path

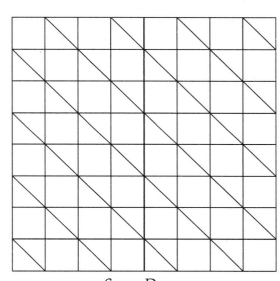

Swan Dance

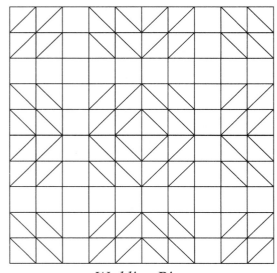

Wedding Ring

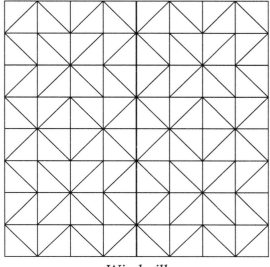

Windmill

All in a Spin

Procedure:

Referring to the block diagrams on the following page, piece 48 blocks. Join the blocks together six across and eight rows down. The outside raw edge of the quilt top is turned under, wrapped around to the back of the quilt and slip-stitched to the backing fabric.

Materials:

Use an assortment of scraps.
Light 5 yds., Dark 5 yds.
Each block is made up of 5 units.

Use Templates:

WW, XX, YY, ZZ, and *AAA.*

Quilt Size:

Approximately 72" X 96"

I.

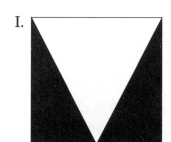

Sew one dark *YY* and one dark *YY(r)* to one light *ZZ* (Make 4).

II.

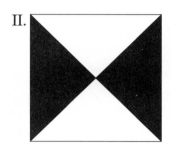

Sew two dark *WW's* to two light *WW's* as shown in the diagram at left (Make 4).

III.

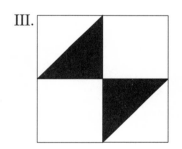

Sew the center square by sewing a dark *XX* to a light *XX* (Make 2), and then sewing each of the *XX's* to a *AAA* square as shown at the left.

IV.

Sew Row 1 as shown in the diagram, making sure the dark and light triangles are turned in the correct orientation.

V.

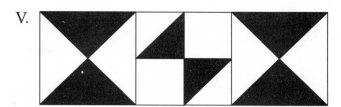

Sew Row 2 as shown in the diagram, making sure of the light and dark orientation of each piece.

VI.

Sew Row 3 according to the above diagram.

VII.

Sew the rows together starting with Row 1 to complete the block.

Pieces per Block:

4 light *ZZ's*, 4 dark *YY's*, 4 dark *YY(r)'s*, 8 dark and 8 light *WW's*, 2 dark and 2 light *XX's*, and 2 light *AAA's*.

Note: Be sure to turn Template YY over to cut YY(r).

Ann's Poinsettia

Procedure:

Referring to the block diagrams on the following page, piece 48 blocks. Join the blocks together six across and eight rows down. The outside raw edge of the quilt top is turned under, wrapped around to the back of the quilt and slip-stitched to the backing fabric.

Materials:

Use an assortment of scraps.
Light 4 1/2 yds., Dark 4 1/2 yds.
Each block is made up of 1 unit.

Quilt Size:

Approximately 72" X 96"

Use Template:

G.

I. 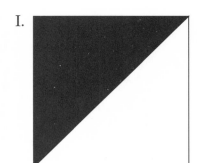 Sew one dark *G* to one light *G* patch (Make 16).

V.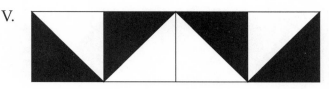

Sew Row 4 according to the above diagram.

VI.

II.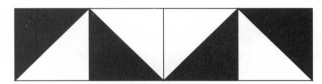

Sew Row 1 together according to the above diagram, making sure to keep the correct orientation of light and dark patches.

Sew the rows together starting with Row 1 and working down to complete the block.

III.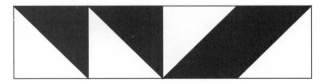

Sew Row 2 together according to the above diagram.

Pieces per Block:

16 dark and 16 light *G's*.

IV.

Sew Row 3, making sure of the correct orientation of the dark and light patches.

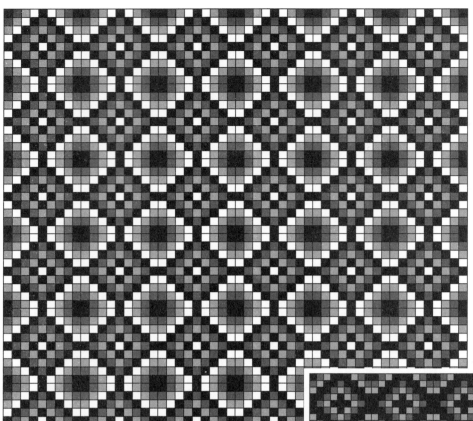

Around the World

Procedure:

Referring to the block diagrams on the following page, piece 48 blocks. Join the blocks together six across and eight rows down. The outside raw edge of the quilt top is turned under, wrapped around to the back of the quilt and slip-stitched to the backing fabric.

Materials:

Use an assortment of scraps.
Light 2 1/4 yds., Dark 3 yds.,
Lighter medium 2 1/2 yds.,
Darker medium 2 1/2 yds.
Each block is made up of 1 unit.

Use Template:

R.

Quilt Size:

Approximately 72" X 96"

I.

Sew four dark pieces to one light piece as shown in the diagram.

II.

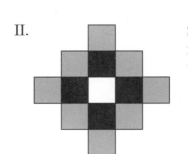

Sew eight lighter medium print pieces to Step I.

III.

Sew twelve darker medium pieces to Step II.

IV.

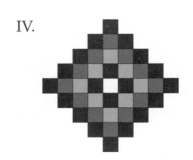

Sew sixteen dark pieces next according to the diagram.

V.

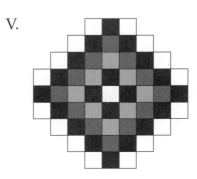

Sew on the sixteen white pieces to Step IV.

VI.

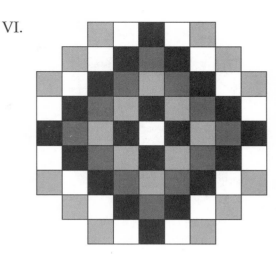

Sew the twelve lighter medium pieces next.

VII.

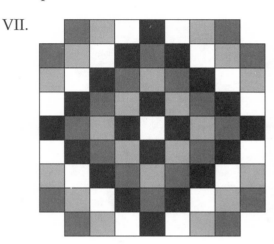

Sew on the eight darker medium pieces as shown in the diagram.

VIII.

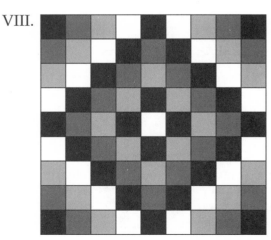

Sew on the dark corners to complete the block.

Pieces per Block:

17 light, 20 lighter medium, 20 darker medium, and 24 dark *R's*.

29

Bear's Paw

Procedure:

Referring to the block diagrams on the following page, piece 48 blocks. Join the blocks together six across and eight rows down. The outside raw edge of the quilt top is turned under, wrapped around to the back of the quilt and slip-stitched to the backing fabric.

Materials:

Use an assortment of scraps.
Light 6 1/4 yds., Dark 6 1/4 yds.
Each block is made up of 5 units.

Use Templates:

RR, SS, TT, UU, and *VV*.

Quilt Size:

Approximately 72" X 96"

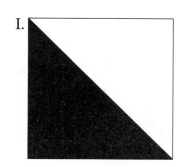

I. Sew one dark *UU* to one light *UU* as shown in the diagram (Make 16).

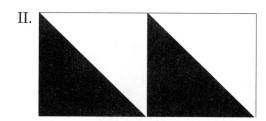

II. Sew two of the Step I's together as shown above (Make 4).

III. Sew two of the Step I's with one *SS* as shown in the diagram, being sure to keep the correct orientation of the light and dark pieces (Make 4).

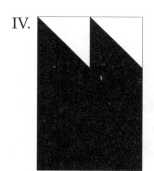

IV. Sew a Step II to a dark *RR* (Make 4).

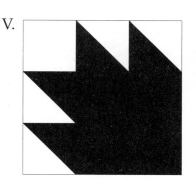

V. Sew one Step III with one Step IV as shown in the diagram (Make 4).

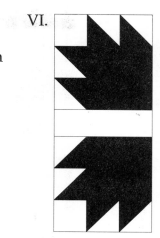

VI. Sew two of the Step V's together according to the diagram at left, using a light *VV* to join the pieces (Make 2).

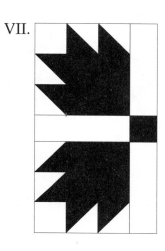

VII. Sew two light *VV's* with one dark *TT* for the vertical center strip and sew to the right side of Step VI.

VIII. Complete the block by rotating a Step VI and sewing to the right side of Step VII.

Pieces per Block:

16 light and 16 dark *UU's*, 4 light *SS's*, 4 dark *RR's*, 4 light *VV's*, and 1 dark *TT*.

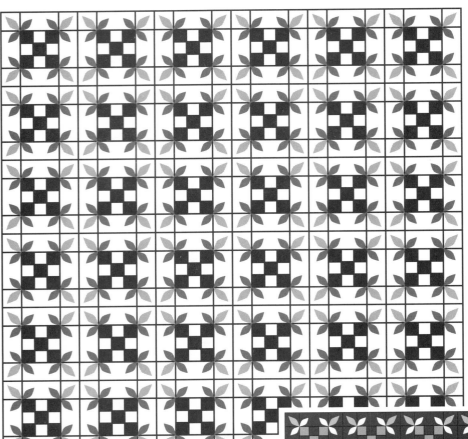

Birds in the Air

Procedure:

Referring to the block diagrams on the following page, piece 48 blocks. Join the blocks together six across and eight rows down. The outside raw edge of the quilt top is turned under, wrapped around to the back of the quilt and slip-stitched to the backing fabric.

Materials:

Use an assortment of scraps.
Light 6 yds., Dark 1 1/4 yds.,
Medium appliqué 1 1/4 yds.,
Dark appliqué 1 3/4 yds.
Each block is made up of 5 units.

Use Templates:

T, S, U, V, and *W*.

Quilt Size:

Approximately 72" X 96"

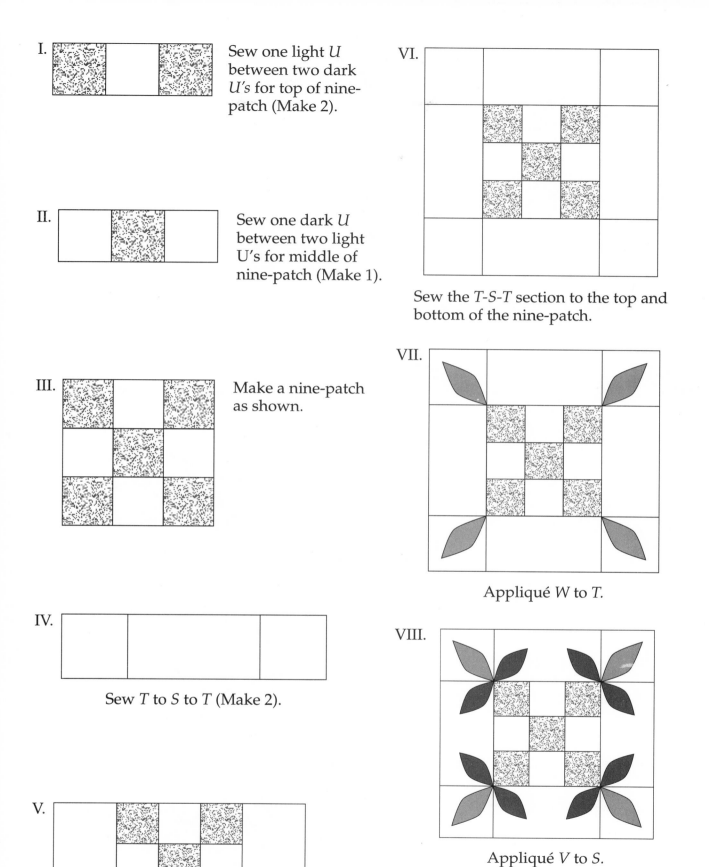

I. Sew one light *U* between two dark *U's* for top of nine-patch (Make 2).

II. Sew one dark *U* between two light *U's* for middle of nine-patch (Make 1).

III. Make a nine-patch as shown.

IV. Sew *T* to *S* to *T* (Make 2).

V. Sew an *S* to each side of the nine-patch.

VI. Sew the *T-S-T* section to the top and bottom of the nine-patch.

VII. Appliqué *W* to *T*.

VIII. Appliqué *V* to *S*.

Pieces per block:

5 medium and 4 light *U's*, 4 light *T's*, 4 light *S's*, 4 medium *W's*, and 8 dark *V's*.

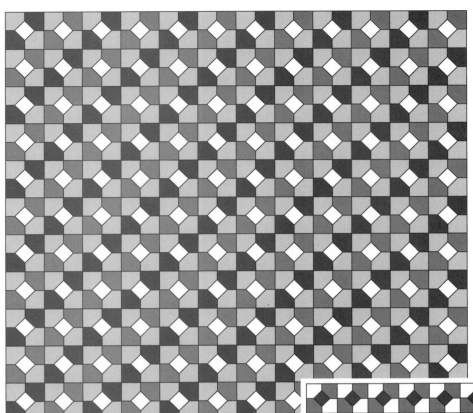

Bow Tie

Procedure:

Referring to the block diagrams on the following page, piece 48 blocks. Join the blocks together six across and eight rows down. The outside raw edge of the quilt top is turned under, wrapped around to the back of the quilt and slip-stitched to the backing fabric.

Materials:

Use an assortment of scraps.
Light 1 yd., Dark 1 3/4 yds.,
Lighter medium 3 1/4 yds., Darker medium 1 3/4 yds.
Each block is made up of 2 units.

Use Templates:

J and I.

Quilt Size:

Approximately 72" X 96"

I.

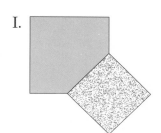

Sew light *J* to a lighter medium *I*.

II.

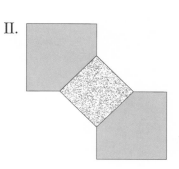

Sew on the second lighter medium *I*.

III.

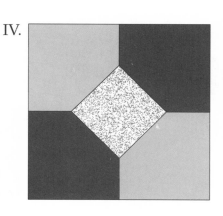

Sew on a dark *I*.

IV.

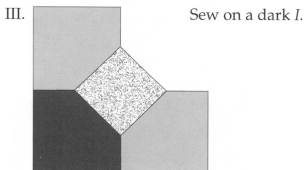

Sew on second dark *I* (Make 2 IV's for each block).

V.

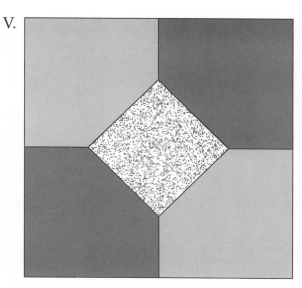

Sew 2 more IV's using a darker medium *I* instead of the dark.

VI.

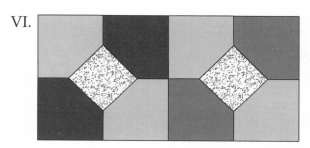

Sew one of the IV's to one of the V's (Make 2).

VII.

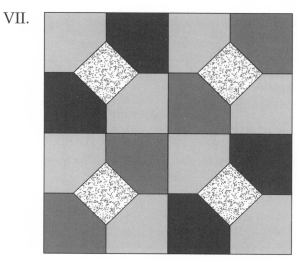

Rotate one of the VI's and sew to the other to complete the block.

Pieces per Block:

4 light *J*'s; 8 lighter medium, 4 darker medium and 4 dark *I*'s.

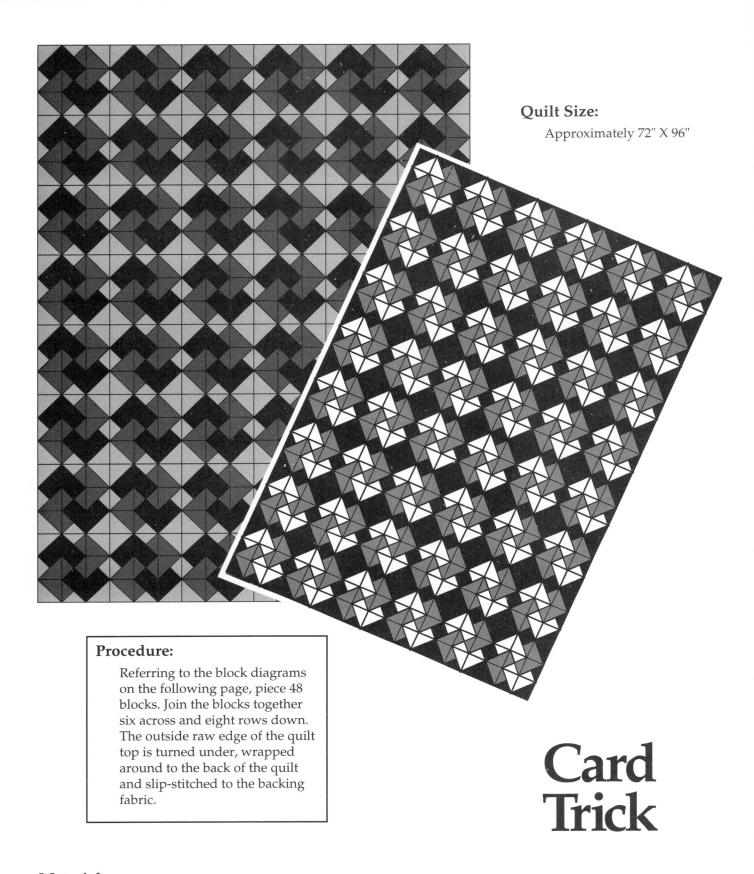

Quilt Size:

Approximately 72" X 96"

Procedure:

Referring to the block diagrams on the following page, piece 48 blocks. Join the blocks together six across and eight rows down. The outside raw edge of the quilt top is turned under, wrapped around to the back of the quilt and slip-stitched to the backing fabric.

Card Trick

Materials:

Use an assortment of scraps.
Light 2 3/4 yds., Dark 2 3/4 yds.,
Medium 2 3/4 yds.
Each block is made up of 2 units.

Use Templates:

P and Q.

36

I.

Sew one dark *P* to one light *P* (Make 2). Then sew one light P to one medium P (Make 2).

II.

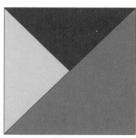

The above sections are made by sewing two *Q's* with one *P*. Make sure to sew dark, medium, and light pieces together as shown (Make 2 of each).

III.

Sew the center section together using the diagram to the left. The *Q* template is used for all pieces (Make 1).

IV.

Sew Row 1 as shown in the diagram, making sure the dark, light and medium triangles are turned in the correct orientation—row is made from one each of Unit I and one Unit IIa.

V.

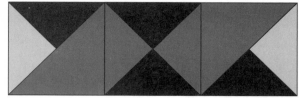

Sew Row 2 together according to the above diagram—two Unit IIb's and one Unit III (the center section).

VI.

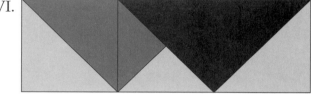

Sew Row 3 according to the above diagram—one each of the Unit I's and one Unit IIa.

VII.

Complete the block by sewing the rows together, in order, from one to three.

Pieces per Block:

4 dark, 4 medium, and 4 light P's; 4 dark, 4 medium, and 4 light Q's.

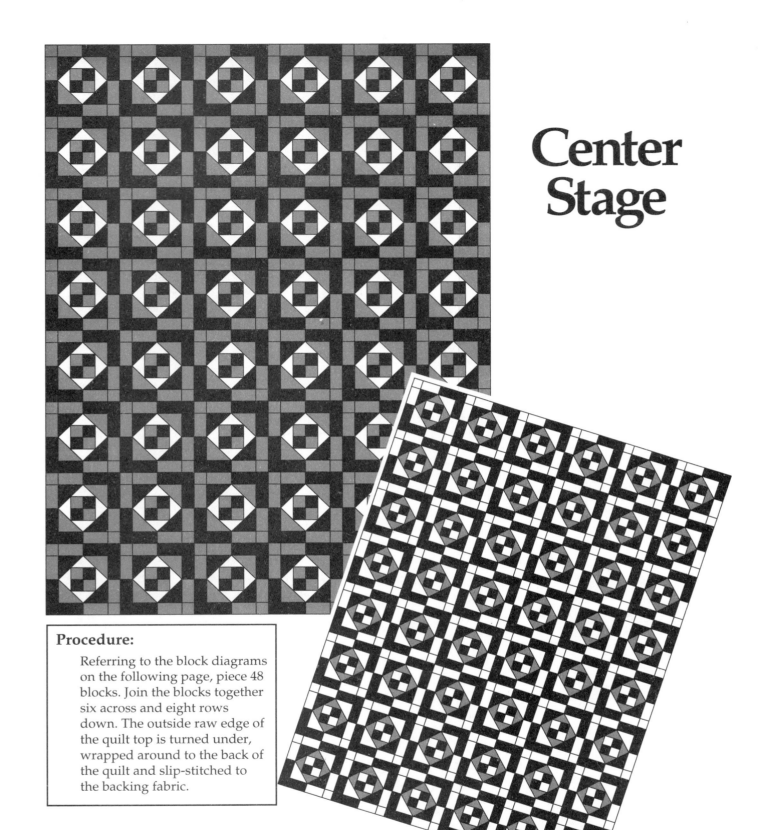

Center Stage

Procedure:

Referring to the block diagrams on the following page, piece 48 blocks. Join the blocks together six across and eight rows down. The outside raw edge of the quilt top is turned under, wrapped around to the back of the quilt and slip-stitched to the backing fabric.

Materials:

Use an assortment of scraps.
Light 1 yd., Dark 3 1/4 yds.,
Medium 3 1/4 yds.
Each block is made up of 4 units.

Use Templates:

GG, HH, II, and *JJ.*

Quilt Size:

Approximately 72" X 96"

I. 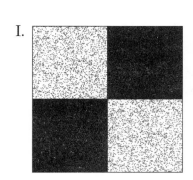 Sew two medium *GG's* to two dark *GG's* using the diagram at left for the correct orientation of dark and light pieces.

V.  Sew the sides of the block by sewing a medium *GG* to a medium *LL*, to a dark *LL*, and then to a dark *GG* (Make 2).

II. 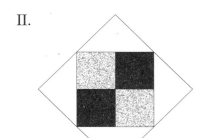 Sew triangle *II's* to Step I as shown.

VI.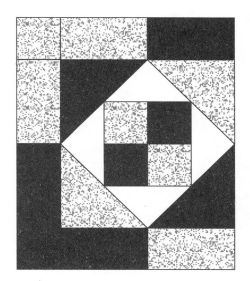

Sew one of the Step V's to the left side of step IV, making sure of the correct orientation.

III. 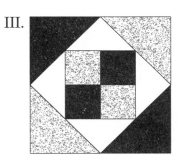 Sew triangle *JJ's* to Step II using the diagram at left to check the correct orientation of medium and dark pieces.

VII.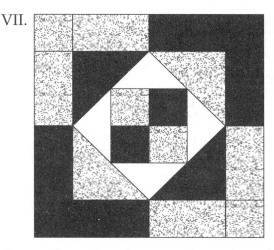

Rotate Step V and sew to the right side to complete the block.

IV. 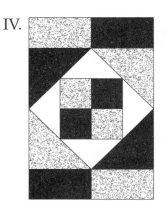 Sew two *HH's* together (Make 2) and attach to the top and bottom of Step III. Use the diagram at left to check the correct orientation of the dark and medium pieces.

Pieces per Block:

4 medium, 4 dark *GG's*; 4 medium, 4 dark *HH's*; 4 light *II's*; 2 medium, and 2 dark *JJ's*.

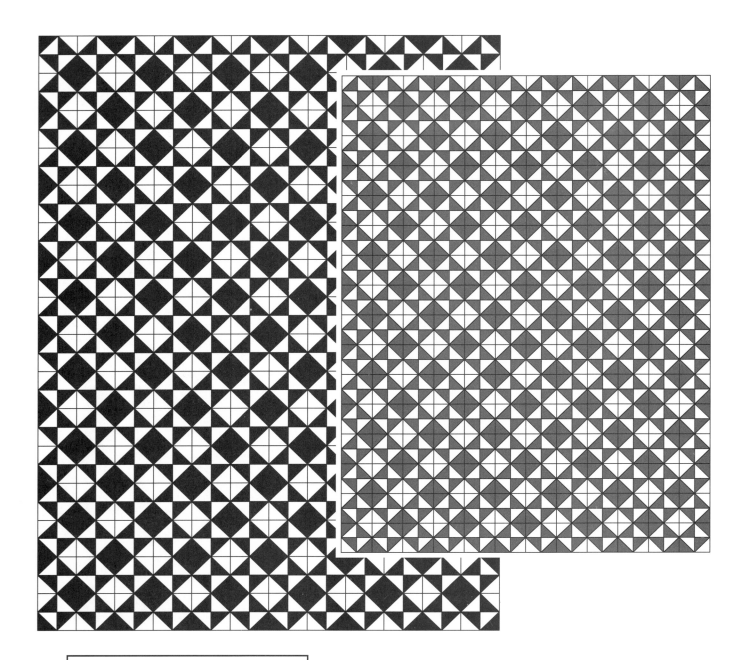

Procedure:

Referring to the block diagrams on the following page, piece 48 blocks. Join the blocks together six across and eight rows down. The outside raw edge of the quilt top is turned under, wrapped around to the back of the quilt and slip-stitched to the backing fabric.

Dorothy's Star

Materials:

Use an assortment of scraps.
Light 4 1/2 yds., Dark 4 1/2 yds.
Each block is made up of 1 unit.

Use Template:

G.

Quilt Size:

Approximately 72" X 96"

I.

Sew one light *G* to one dark *G* (Make 16).

V.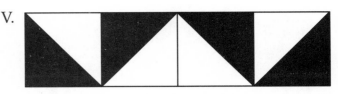

Sew Row 4 as shown in the above diagram.

II.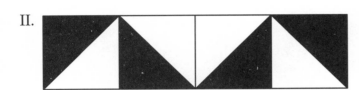

Sew Row 1 using the above diagram to insure that the light and dark pieces are in the correct orientation.

VI.

Sew the rows together in order from one to four to complete the block.

Pieces per Block:

16 light and 16 dark *G*'s.

III.

Sew Row 2 according to the above diagram making sure of the correct orientation of the pieces.

IV.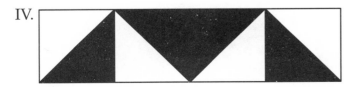

Sew Row 3 as shown in the diagram, making sure the dark and light triangles are turned in the correct orientation.

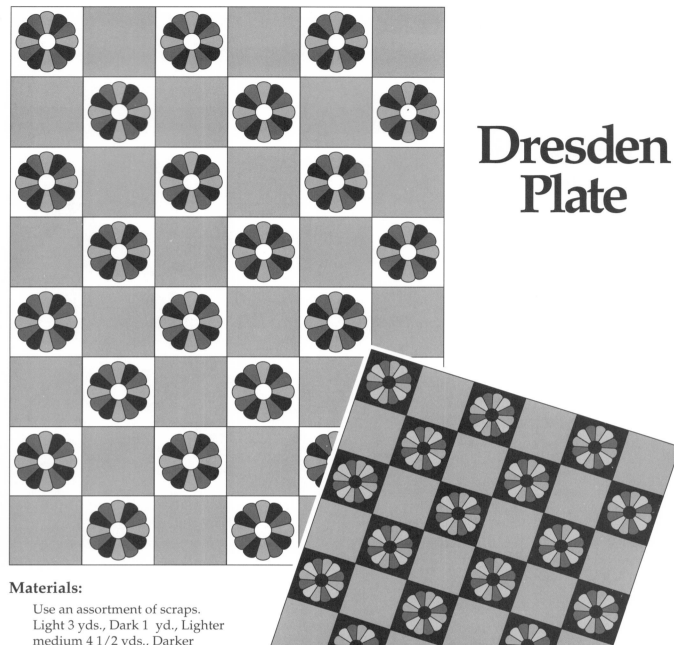

Dresden Plate

Materials:

Use an assortment of scraps.
Light 3 yds., Dark 1 yd., Lighter
medium 4 1/2 yds., Darker
medium 1 1/2 yds.
Each block is made up of 2 units.

Procedure:

Referring to the block diagrams
on the following page, piece 24
blocks. Alternating Dresden
Plate blocks with plain 12 1/2"
squares, join the blocks together
six across and eight rows down.
The outside raw edge of the
quilt top is turned under,
wrapped around to the back of
the quilt and slip-stitched to the
backing fabric.

Use Templates:

A and *E*.

Quilt Size:

Approximately 72" X 96"

I.

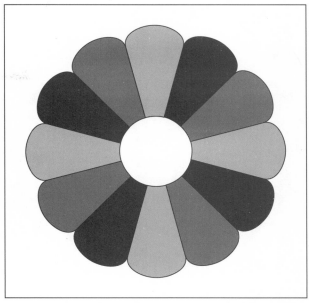

Sew two *E's* together, starting at the small end and sewing to the dots on the template.

III.

Appliqué Step II to a 12 1/2" background fabric. Make sure that the appliqué is centered.

II.

Sew the other *E's* in place to form a circle—12 *E's* are needed per block.

IV.

To complete the block appliqué the center circle *A* to Step III.

Pieces per Block:

1 light A; 4 lighter medium, 4 darker medium, and 4 dark E's.
Cut 24 light and 24 lighter medium blocks, 12 1/2" square.

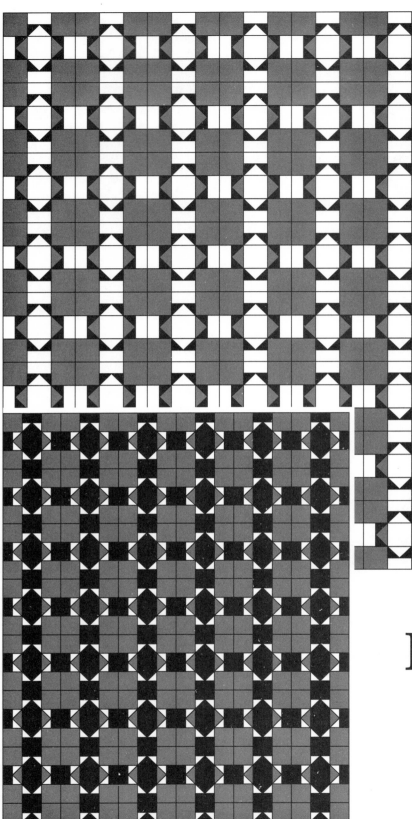

Procedure:

Referring to the block diagrams on the following page, piece 48 blocks. Join the blocks together six across and eight rows down. The outside raw edge of the quilt top is turned under, wrapped around to the back of the quilt and slip-stitched to the backing fabric.

Pieces per Block:

1 light, 4 medium OO's; 4 light NN's; 2 light, 2 medium Q's; and 8 dark XX's.

Friendship Album

Materials:

Use an assortment of scraps. Light 3 1/2 yds., Dark 1 1/4 yd., Medium 3 3/4 yds. Each block is made up of 4 units.

Quilt Size:

Approximately 72" X 96"

Use Templates:

OO, NN, Q, and XX.

I.

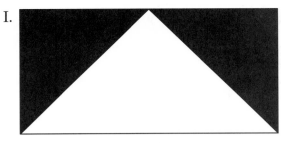

Sew two dark *XX's* to one light *Q* (Make 2).

II.

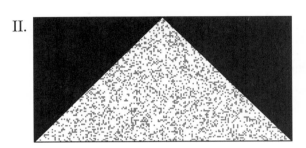

Sew two dark *XX's* to one medium *Q* (Make 2).

III.

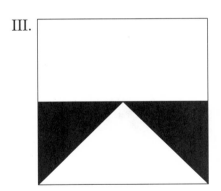

Sew one Step I to one light *NN* (Make 2).

IV.

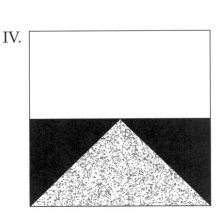

Sew one Step II to one light *NN* (Make 2).

V.

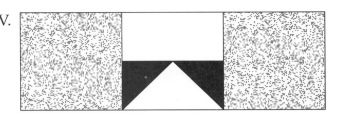

Sew Row 1 as shown in the diagram (using *OO* pieces for the corners), making sure of the light and dark orientation of each piece.

VI.

Sew Row 2 as shown in the diagram, making sure of the light and dark orientation of each piece.

VII.

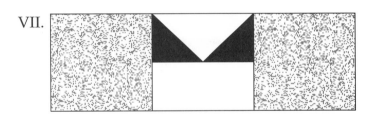

Sew Row 3 according to the above diagram.

VIII.

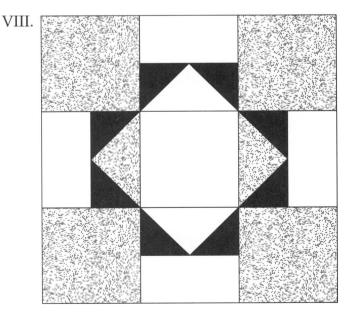

Sew the rows together to complete the block.

Garden Path

Procedure:

Referring to the block diagrams on the following page, piece 48 blocks. Join the blocks together six across and eight rows down. The outside raw edge of the quilt top is turned under, wrapped around to the back of the quilt and slip-stitched to the backing fabric.

Materials:

Use an assortment of scraps. Light 4 1/2 yds., Dark 4 1/2 yd. Each block is made up of 1 unit.

Use Template:

G.

Quilt Size:

Approximately 72" X 96"

I.

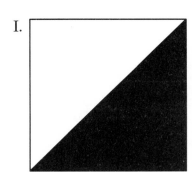

Sew one light *G* to one dark *G* (Make 16).

V.

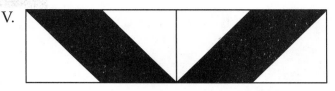

Sew Row 4 as shown in the above diagram.

II.

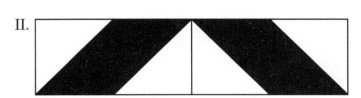

Sew Row 1 using the above diagram to insure that the light and dark pieces are in the correct orientation.

VI.

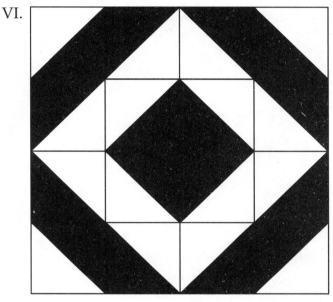

Sew the rows together in order from one to four to complete the block.

III.

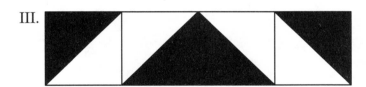

Sew Row 2 according to the above diagram, making sure of the correct orientation of the pieces.

Pieces per Block:

16 light and 16 dark *G's*.

IV.

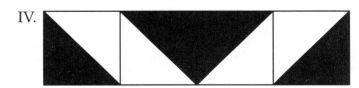

Sew Row 3 as shown in the diagram, making sure the dark and light triangles are turned in the correct orientation.

Gold Mine

Procedure:

Referring to the block diagrams on the following page, piece 48 blocks. Join the blocks together six across and eight rows down. The outside raw edge of the quilt top is turned under, wrapped around to the back of the quilt and slip-stitched to the backing fabric.

Materials:

Use an assortment of scraps.
Light 4 1/2 yds., Dark 3 1/2 yds.
Each block is made up of 3 units.

Use Templates:

OO, PP, and QQ.

Quilt Size:

Approximately 72" X 96"

I. 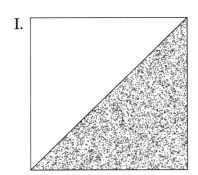 Sew one dark *QQ* to one light *QQ* (Make 4).

V.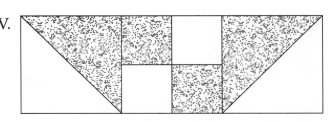

Sew Row 3 together according to the above diagram, making sure to keep the right orientation of the light and dark pieces.

II. 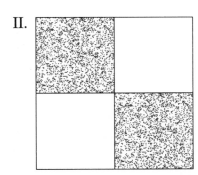 Sew four *PP's* together as shown in the diagram. (Make 4).

VI.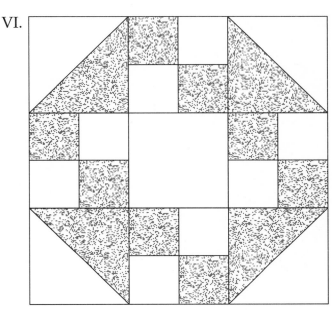

III.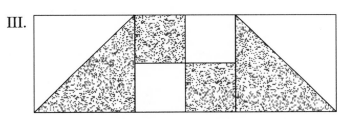

Sew Row 1 together according to the above diagram, making sure to keep the right orientation of the light and dark pieces.

Complete the block by sewing the rows together, starting with Row 1 and working down.

Pieces per Block:

1 light *OO*; 8 light, 8 dark *PP's*; 4 light and 4 dark *QQ's*.

IV.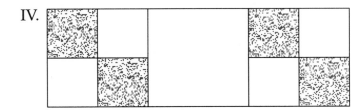

Sew Row 2 as shown in the diagram, using 2 of the Step II pieces and one light *OO*.

Quilt Size:

Approximately 79" X 92"

Use Template:

H

Pieces per Block:

1 light, 6 medium, and 12 dark *H's*.
Cut 672 light and 268 dark *H's* for background.

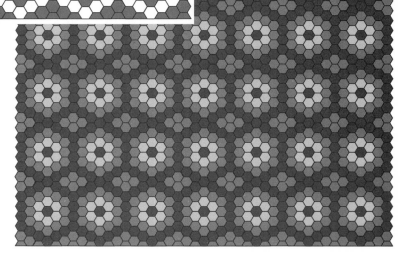

Procedure:

Referring to the block diagrams on the following page, piece 49 blocks. Join the blocks together with the light and dark background pieces, seven blocks across and seven rows down. The edges can be trimmed or left scalloped. The outside raw edge of the quilt top is turned under, wrapped around to the back of the quilt and slip-stitched to the backing fabric.

Grandmother's Flower Garden

Materials:

Use an assortment of scraps.
Light 4 3/4 yds., Dark 5 1/4 yds., Medium 2 yds.
Each block is made up of 1 unit.

I.

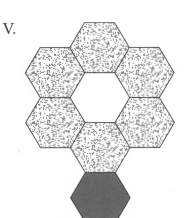

Start the block with a light piece.

II.

Sew a medium piece to the bottom of the light center.

III.

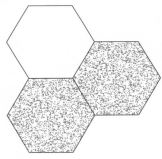

Continue to add medium pieces to the center, working in a counterclockwise direction.

IV.

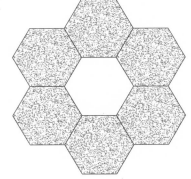

Complete the sewing of the medium pieces.

V.

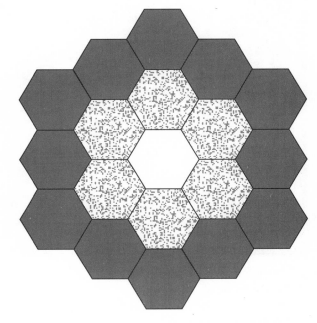

Sew the next row using dark pieces and working in a counterclockwise direction as with the previous row.

VI.

Complete the block by sewing on the other dark pieces.

VII.

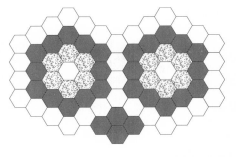

Piece the blocks together with light pieces, referring to the illustration on the previous page. Fill the open spaces with four dark pieces in the form of a diamond.

Granny's Diamond

Procedure:

Referring to the block diagrams on the following page, piece 28 diamond blocks. Join 16 blocks together for the center, using the above diagram as a reference. Using a pieced diamond block as a pattern, trace around and cut out a solid block pattern. Cut 18 full-size diamonds and 12 half diamonds, adding 1/4" seam allowance to the top of the halves. Sew the center, the plain blocks, and the remaining pieced blocks together, following the above diagram. Trim the side edges, cutting the pieced edge blocks in half vertically. See the general instruction section at the beginning of this book for the instructions for borders and binding. The inside (dark) border is 2 1/2" wide (including the seam allowance) and the lighter outside border is 3 1/2" (including the seam allowance). The quilt top was finished with a commercial binding that was purchased after the quilting was completed and the finished dimensions measured.

Materials:

Use an assortment of dark and light scraps.
1/2 yd. each makes 3 diamond blocks), 3 1/2 yds. are used for the background.
Use 1/2 yd. for the 2 1/2" dark border if a 44" material is pieced for it. Use 1 yd. if the outside binding is also made of this material.
The 3 1/2" border uses 3/4 yd.
Each block is made up of 2 units.

Use Templates:

N and O.

Quilt Size:

Approximately 70" X 82"

I.

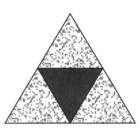

Sew three light *O's* and one dark *O* together (Make 12).

II.

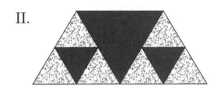

Sew two of the Step I units with one *N* to make this section (Make 2).

III.

Sew three of the Step I's with 2 *N's* (Make 2).

IV.

Sew Center by rotating one of the Step III's and sewing to the other.

V.

Sew I and II together and attach to the top of Step IV.

VI.

Sew the other set of I's and II's together and attach to the bottom of Step IV in order to complete the block.

Pieces per Block:

6 dark *N's*; 36 light and 12 dark *O's*.

Hands All Around

Use Templates:

Y, Z, AA, BB, and CC.

Materials:

Use an assortment of scraps.
Light 3 1/2 yds., Dark 6 yds.
2 1/2 yds. light and 1/2 yd.
dark for sashing.
Each block is made up of 5
units.

Quilt Size:

Approximately 78" X 93"

Procedure:

Referring to the block diagrams on the following page, piece 30 blocks.
Join the blocks together five across and six rows down. The quilt above has
a sashing that is 3 1/2" wide including the seam allowance. It has no separate binding.

The two quilts pictured at the bottom have 20 blocks and a border. The
outside raw edge of the quilt top is turned under, wrapped around to the
back of the quilt and slip-stitched to the backing fabric.

I.

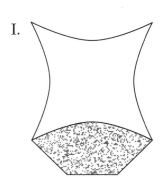

Sew Y and Z together. Clip curved seam allowances and press away from the center section.

II.

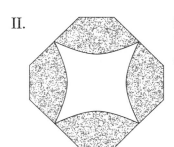

Sew the remaining Z's to Y. This piece should be a flat octagon.

III.

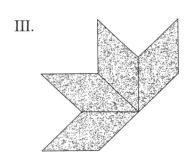

Join four diamonds (Template AA) for each of the corners of the block (Make 4).

IV.

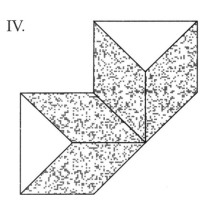

Sew triangle BB's to the AA's.

V.

Sew the AA-BB's of Step IV to the Y-Z piece of Step II.

VI.

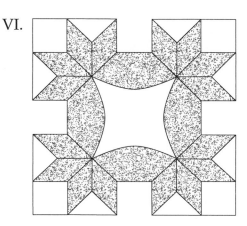

Sew in corner squares.

VII.

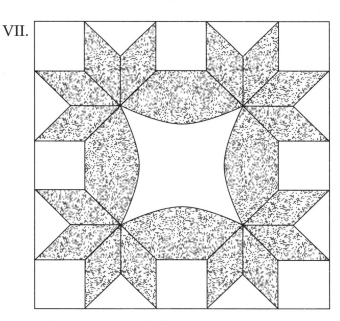

Sew in the middle squares last to make a perfectly square block.

Pieces per Block:

1 light Y; 4 dark Z's; 16 dark AA's; 8 light BB's; and 8 light CC's.

For sashing, cut 71 strips 3 1/2" by 12 1/2" from light and 42 squares 3 1/2" by 3 1/2" from dark.

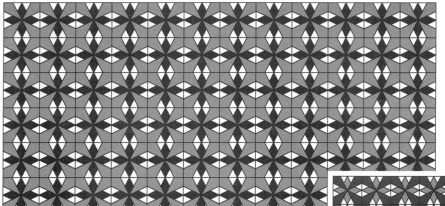

Hattie's
Choice

Procedure:

Referring to the block diagrams on the following page, piece 48 blocks. Join the blocks together six across and eight rows down. The outside raw edge of the quilt top is turned under, wrapped around to the back of the quilt and slip-stitched to the backing fabric.

Use Templates:

K, L, and M.

Quilt Size:

Approximately 72" X 96"

Materials:

Use an assortment of scraps.
Light 3 1/2 yds., Dark 2 3/4 yds.,
Medium 4 3/4 yds.
Each block is made up of 3 units.

I.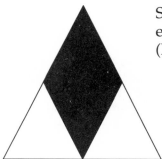

Sew one light *K* to each side of a dark *M* (Make 16).

V.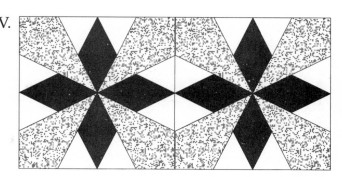

Sew two of the Step IV quarter blocks together to make this half block (Make 2).

II.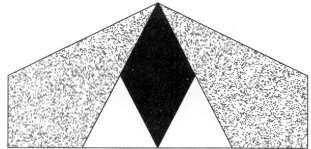

Sew the two *L's* in place as shown in the diagram.

III.

Sew one of the other Step I's in place as shown (Make 8).

VI.

Sew two of the half blocks together to complete the block.

Pieces per Block:

32 light K's; 16 medium L's, and 16 dark M's.

IV.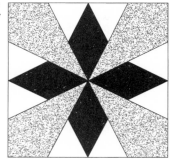

Rotate one of the Step III's and sew to another to make a quarter block (Make 4).

Honey Bee

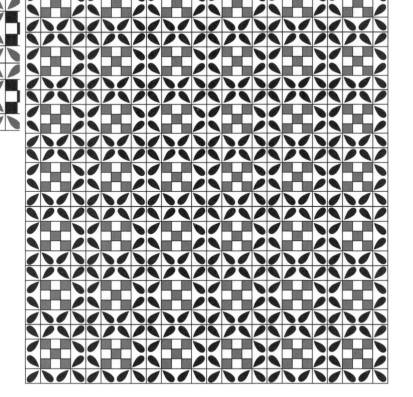

Procedure:

Referring to the block diagrams on the following page, piece 48 blocks. Join the blocks together six across and eight rows down. The outside raw edge of the quilt top is turned under, wrapped around to the back of the quilt and slip-stitched to the backing fabric.

Materials:

Use an assortment of scraps.
Light 6 yds., Dark 1 1/4 yds.,
Appliqué 3 1/2 yds.
Each block is made up of 4 units.

Use Templates:

T, S, U, and *X.*

Quilt Size:

Approximately 72" X 96"

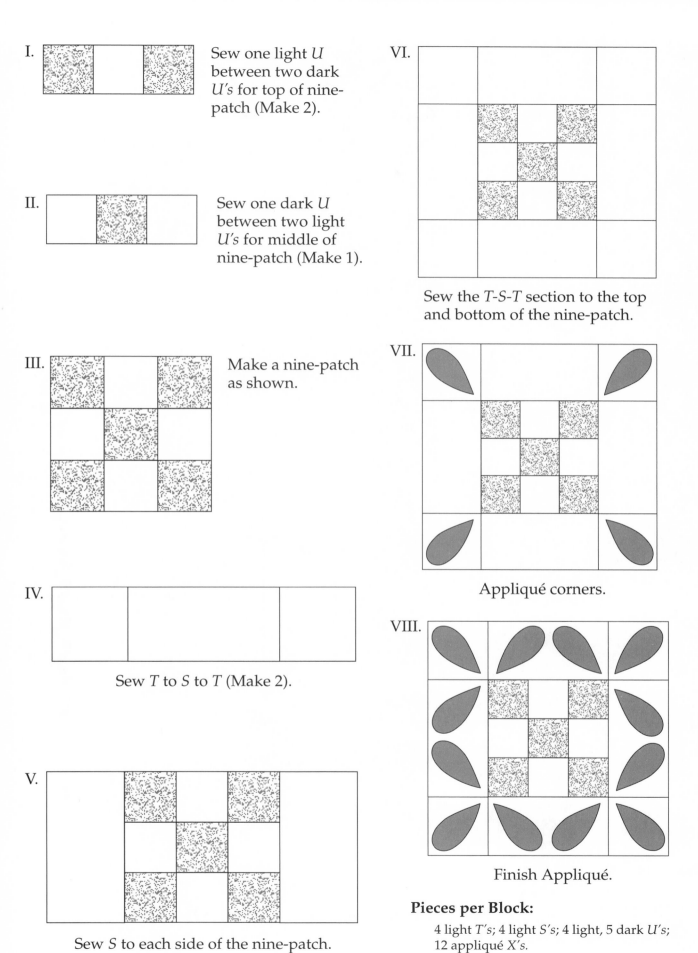

I. Sew one light *U* between two dark *U's* for top of nine-patch (Make 2).

II. Sew one dark *U* between two light *U's* for middle of nine-patch (Make 1).

III. Make a nine-patch as shown.

IV. Sew *T* to *S* to *T* (Make 2).

V. Sew *S* to each side of the nine-patch.

VI. Sew the *T-S-T* section to the top and bottom of the nine-patch.

VII. Appliqué corners.

VIII. Finish Appliqué.

Pieces per Block:

4 light *T's*; 4 light *S's*; 4 light, 5 dark *U's*; 12 appliqué *X's*.

59

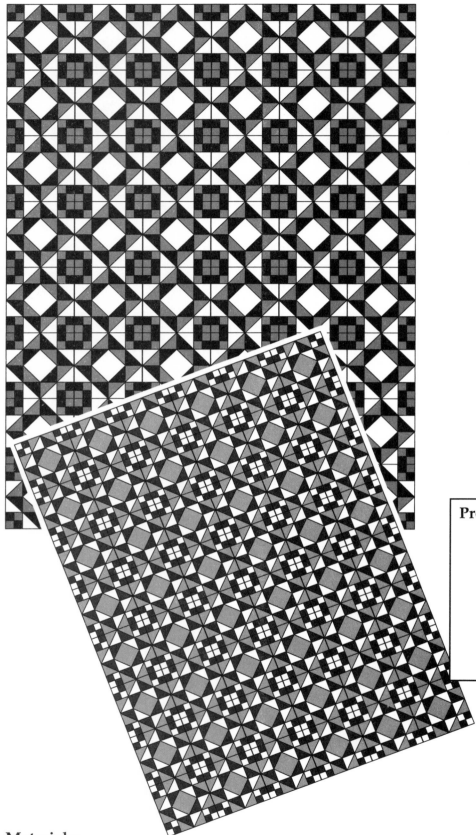

Merry-Go-Round

Pieces per Block:

8 light, 6 medium, 6 dark *DD's*; 1 light *EE*; 8 medium, and 8 dark *FF's*.

Procedure:

Referring to the block diagrams on the following page, piece 48 blocks. Join the blocks together six across and eight rows down. The outside raw edge of the quilt top is turned under, wrapped around to the back of the quilt and slip-stitched to the backing fabric.

Materials:

Use an assortment of scraps.
Light 3 1/2 yds., Dark 3 yds.,
Medium 3 yds.
Each block is made up of 3 units.

Use Templates:

DD, *EE*, and *FF*.

Quilt Size:

Approximately 72" X 96"

I.  Sew one medium *FF* to one dark *FF* (Make 8).

II.  Rotate a Step I piece and sew to another to complete the corners (Make 4).

III.  Sew a light *DD* to a medium *DD*. Sew a light *DD* to a dark *DD*. (Make 4 of each).

IV.  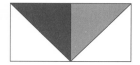 Sew the pieces from Step III together using the above diagrams (Make 2 of each).

V. 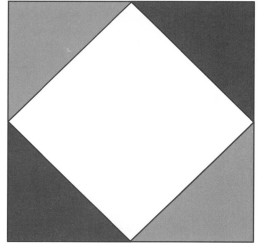 Sew the center section using the above diagram, being sure to line up the dots on *DD* to those on *EE*.

VI.  Sew two of the Step IV's to the center section using the diagram at left to insure correct orientation of the dark and medium pieces. Make sure to line up the center of the Step IV's with the point of the white center.

VII.  Sew the left row together and then sew it to Step VI, making sure to line up the center of the row with a point of the white center square.

VIII.  Sew the right row together according to the above diagram and attach to Step VII.

61

Monkey Wrench

Procedure:

Referring to the block diagrams on the following page, piece 30 blocks. For the sashing, cut 2 1/2"-wide strips (includes seam allowance). Join the blocks together five across and six rows down, with sashing between blocks and rows.

The outside raw edge of the quilt top is turned under, wrapped around to the back of the quilt and slip-stitched to the backing fabric. The quilt pictured at right has 48 blocks and no sashing. It is approximately 72" X 96".

Materials:

Use an assortment of scraps.
Light 2 1/4 yds., Dark 1 yd.,
Medium 3/4 yd., Sashing 2 1/4 yds.
Each block is made up of 3 units.

Quilt Size:

Approximately 72" X 86"

Use Templates:

OO, NN, and *QQ*.

I.

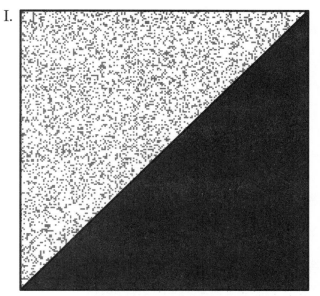

Sew a dark and a light *QQ* together (Make 4).

II.

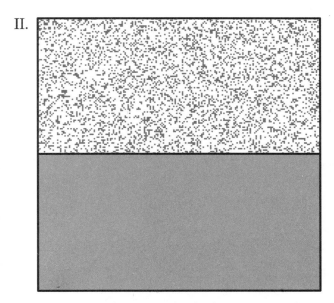

Sew a medium and a light *NN* together (Make 4).

III.

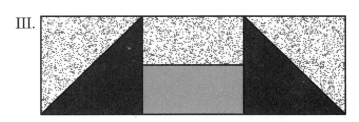

Sew Row 1 together following the above diagram.

IV.

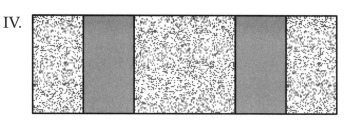

Sew two Step II's to *OO* in order to make Row 2.

V.

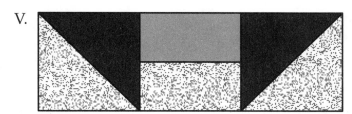

Sew Row 3 according to the above diagram.

VI.

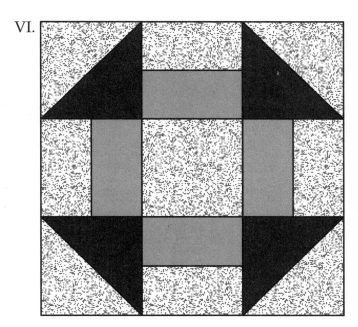

Sew the Rows together to complete the block.

Pieces per Block:

4 light, 4 medium *NN's*; 1 light *OO*; 4 light, and 4 dark *QQ's*.

Night Light

Procedure:

Referring to the block diagrams on the following page, piece 48 blocks. Join the blocks together six across and eight rows down. The outside raw edge of the quilt top is turned under, wrapped around to the back of the quilt and slip-stitched to the backing fabric.

Quilt Size:

Approximately 72" X 96"

Use Template:

G.

Materials:

Use an assortment of scraps. Light 5 yds., Dark 2 1/2 yds., Medium 2 1/2 yds. Each block is made up of 1 unit.

I.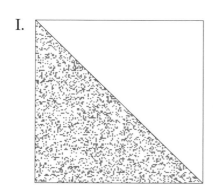

Sew one light *G* to one medium *G* (Make 8).

V.

Sew Row 3 according to the above diagram.

II.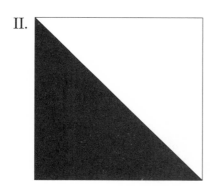

Sew one light *G* to one dark *G* (Make 8).

VI.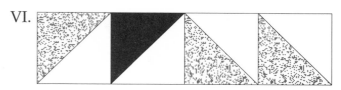

Sew Row 4 according to the above diagram.

III.

Sew Row 1 as shown in the diagram, making sure the dark and light tringles are turned in the correct orientation.

VII.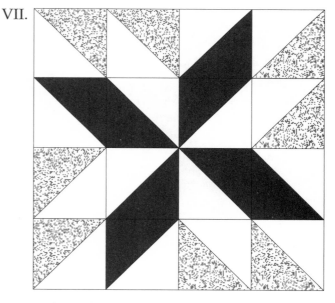

Sew the Rows together, starting with Row 1, to complete the block.

Pieces per Block:

16 light, 8 medium, and 8 dark *G's.*

IV.

Sew Row 2 as shown in the diagram, making sure of the dark and light orientation of each piece.

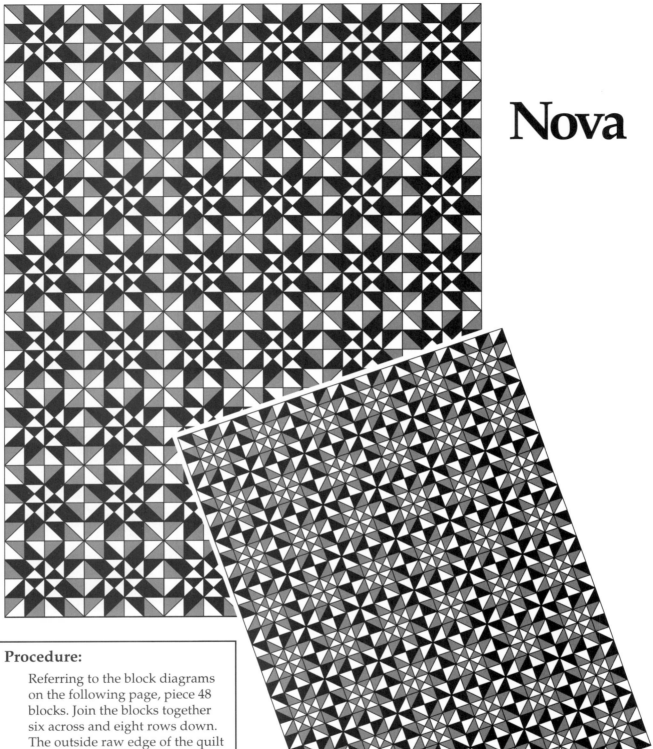

Nova

Procedure:

Referring to the block diagrams on the following page, piece 48 blocks. Join the blocks together six across and eight rows down. The outside raw edge of the quilt top is turned under, wrapped around to the back of the quilt and slip-stitched to the backing fabric.

Materials:

Use an assortment of scraps.
Light 4 yds., Dark 4 yds.,
Medium 2 1/2 yds.
Each block is made up of 2 units.

Use Templates:
C and G.

Quilt Size:
Approximately 72" X 96"

I.

Sew triangle *G's* together as shown—light to medium, light to dark and medium to dark (Make 4 of each).

II.

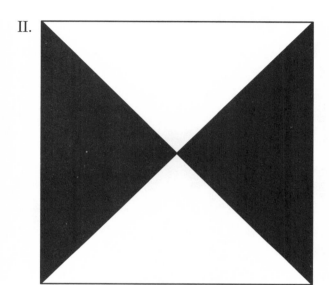

Sew light and dark *C's* together as shown (Make 4).

III.

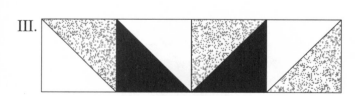

Sew Row 1 together using the above diagram to check the correct orientation of the light, medium and dark triangles.

IV.

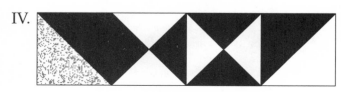

Sew Row 2 as shown in the diagram, making sure the dark and light triangles are turned in the correct orientation.

V.

Sew Row 3 as shown in the diagram, making sure of the orientation of each piece.

VI.

Sew Row 4 according to the above diagram.

VII.

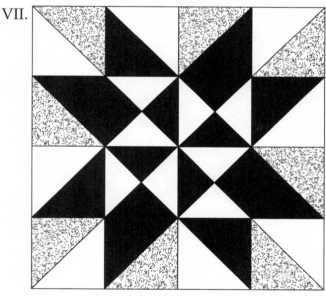

Sew the block together from Row 1 down.

Pieces per Block:

8 light, 8 dark *C's*; 8 light, 8 medium, and 8 dark *G's*.

Pinwheel

Procedure:

Referring to the block diagrams on the following page, piece 48 blocks. Join the blocks together six across and eight rows down. The outside raw edge of the quilt top is turned under, wrapped around to the back of the quilt and slip-stitched to the backing fabric.

Materials:

Use an assortment of scraps.
Light 3 3/4 yds., Dark 2 1/2 yds., Lighter medium 2 1/4 yds., Darker medium 2 1/4 yds.
Each block is made up of 2 units.

Use Templates:

B and *G.*

Quilt Size:

Approximately 72" X 96"

I.

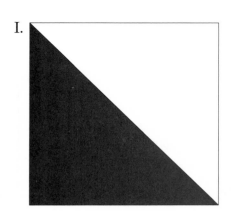

Sew one dark *G* to one light *G* (Make 8).

II.

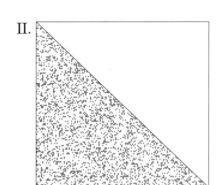

Sew one darker medium *G* to one light *G* (Make 2).

III.

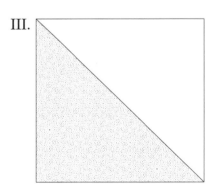

Sew one ligher medium *G* to one light *G* (Make 2).

IV.

Sew Row 1 as shown in the diagram, making sure the dark and light triangles are turned in the correct orientation.

V.

Sew Row 2 as shown in the diagram, making sure of the light and dark orientation of each piece.

VI.

Sew Row 3 according to the above diagram.

VII.

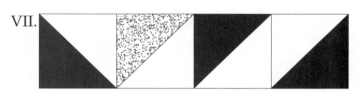

Sew Row 4 according to the above diagram.

VIII.

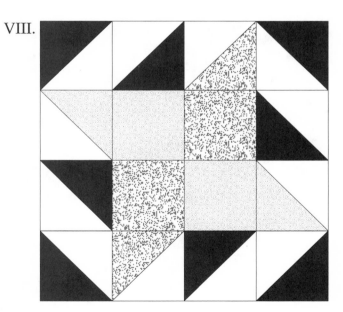

Sew the rows together, starting at Row 1 and working down, to complete the block.

Pieces per Block:

2 lighter medium, 2 darker medium *B's*; 12 light, 2 lighter medium, 2 darker medium, and 8 dark *G's.*

Procedure:

Referring to the block diagrams on the following page, piece 48 blocks. Join the blocks together six across and eight rows down. The outside raw edge of the quilt top is turned under, wrapped around to the back of the quilt and slip-stitched to the backing fabric.

Poinsettia

Materials:

Use an assortment of scraps.
Light 3 3/4 yds., Dark 2 1/2 yds.,
Lighter medium 1 1/4 yds., Darker
medium 2 1/2 yds.
Each block is made up of 1 unit.

Use Template:

G.

Quilt Size:

Approximately 72" X 96"

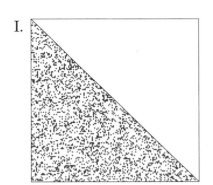

I. Sew one light *G* to one darker medium *G* (Make 8).

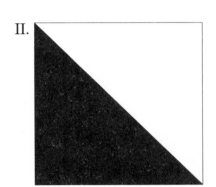

II. Sew one light *G* to one dark *G* (Make 4).

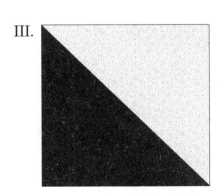

III. Sew one lighter medium *G* to one dark *G* (Make 4).

IV. Sew Row 1 as shown in the diagram, making sure the dark and light triangles are turned in the correct orientation.

V. Sew Row 2 as shown in the diagram, making sure of the light and dark orientation of each piece.

VI. Sew Row 3 according to the above diagram.

VII. Sew Row 4 according to the above diagram.

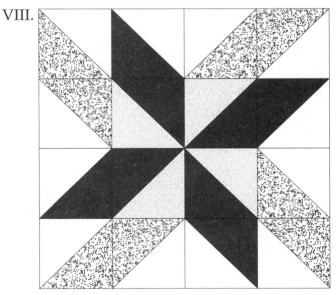

VIII. Sew the rows together, starting with Row 1, to complete the block.

Pieces per Block:

12 light, 4 lighter medium, 8 darker medium, and 8 dark *G*'s.

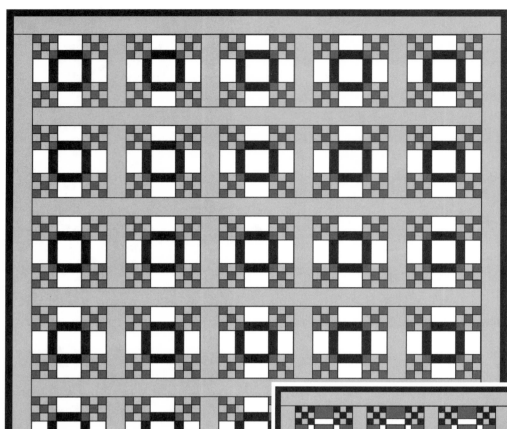

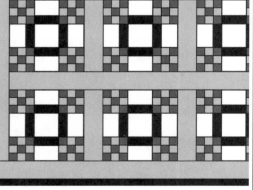

Puss in the Corner

Use Templates:

KK, LL, MM, and *OO.*

Quilt Size:

Approximately 78" X 93"

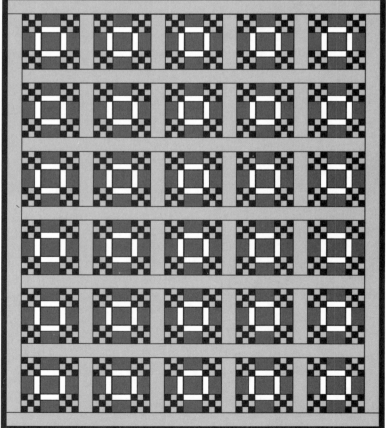

Procedure:

Referring to the block diagrams on the following page, piece 30 blocks. Join the blocks together five across and six rows down using 3 1/2 inch sashing (includes seam allowance). The border is also made of 3 1/2 inch strips. The binding is made of 3 inch strips pressed in half lengthwise with wrong side touching. With raw edge of binding even with raw edge of quilt top, sew binding in place. Turn folded edge to back and blind stitch in place.

Materials:

Use an assortment of scraps.
Light 2 1/4 yds., Dark 1 yd., Lighter medium 1 1/2 yds., Darker medium 1 3/4 yds., Sashing and Border 2 3/4 yds., Binding 1 yd. Each block is made up of 4 units.

I.

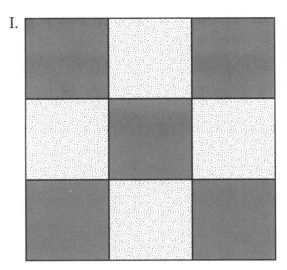

Sew a nine patch with template *LL* according to the above diagram (Make 4).

II.

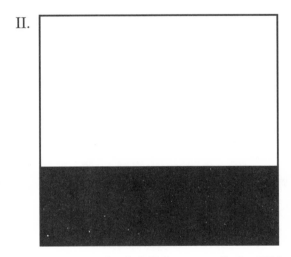

Sew one dark MM to one light KK (Make 4).

III.

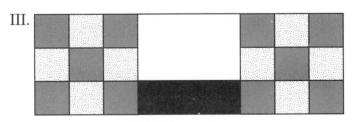

Sew Row 1 together according to the above diagram, making sure of the correct orientation of the dark and light pieces.

IV.

Sew Row 2 together by rotating two Step II's (as shown in the diagram) and sewing them to each side of template *OO*.

V.

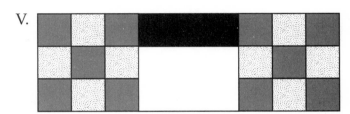

Sew Row 3 together according to the above diagram.

VI.

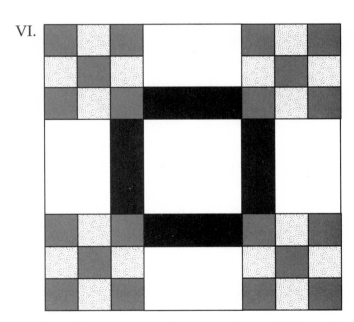

Sew the rows together, starting with Row 1 and working down, in order to complete the block.

Pieces per Block:

4 light *KK's*; 16 lighter medium, 20 darker medium *LL's*; 4 dark *MM's*; 1 light *OO*.
For sashing, cut 24 strips 3 1/2" by 12 1/2" and seven 3 1/2"-wide strips the width of the quilt. Cut two side borders 3 1/2" wide.

Procedure:

Referring to the block diagrams on the following page, piece 48 blocks. Join the blocks together six across and eight rows down. The outside raw edge of the quilt top is turned under, wrapped around to the back of the quilt and slip-stitched to the backing fabric.

Road with No End

Materials:

Use an assortment of scraps.
Light 1 yd., Dark 3 1/4 yds.,
Medium 3 1/4 yds.
Each block is made up of 2 units.

Use Templates:

GG and *HH*.

Quilt Size:

Approximately 72" X 96"

I.

Sew one light *GG* to one dark *HH*. Make sure to stop sewing the light *GG* a quarter inch from the bottom in order to provide the necessary seam allowance.

II.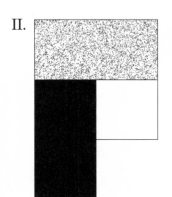

Sew a medium *HH* to the top of Step I.

III.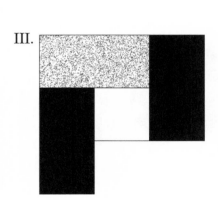

Sew a dark *HH* to Step II as shown in the diagram.

IV.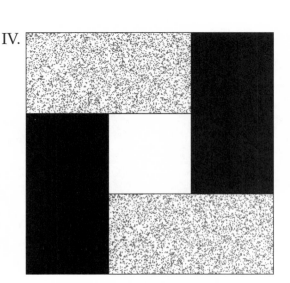

Complete the quarter block piece by sewing a medium *HH* to Step III (Make 4).

V.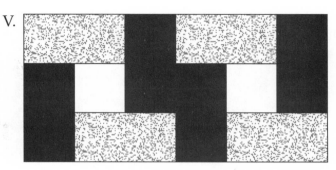

Sew two of the Step IV's together as shown (Make 2).

VI.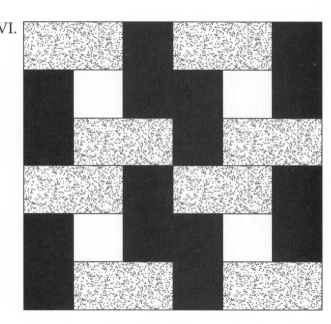

Sew two of the Step V's together in order to complete the block.

Pieces per Block:
4 light GG's; 8 medium and 8 dark *HH's*.

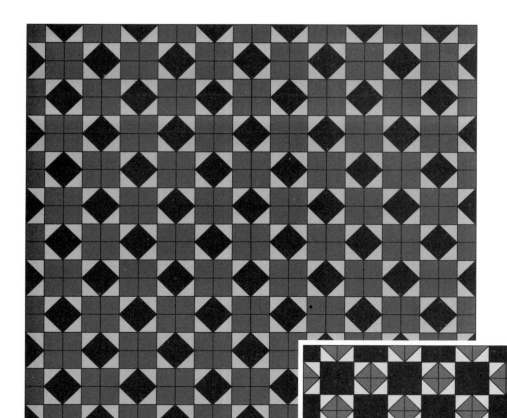

Stone Path

Procedure:

Referring to the block diagrams on the following page, piece 48 blocks. Join the blocks together six across and eight rows down. The outside raw edge of the quilt top is turned under, wrapped around to the back of the quilt and slip-stitched to the backing fabric.

Materials:

Use an assortment of scraps.
Light 2 1/4 yds., Dark 2 1/4 yds.,
Medium 3 1/4 yds.
Each block is made up of 2 units.

Use Templates:

B and G.

Quilt Size:

Approximately 72" X 96"

I.

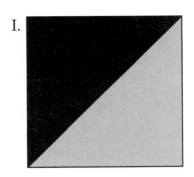

Sew one dark *G* to one light *G* (Make 8).

V.

Sew Row 4 according to the above diagram.

II.

Sew Row 1 as shown in the diagram, making sure the dark and light triangles are turned in the correct orientation.

VI.

Complete the block by sewing the rows together in order from 1 to 4.

III.

Sew Row 2 according to the above diagram.

Pieces per Block:

8 light, 8 dark *G's*; and 8 medium *B's*.

IV.

Sew Row 3 together, making sure of the correct orientation of the light and dark triangles.

Swan Dance

Procedure:

Referring to the block diagrams on the following page, piece 48 blocks. Join the blocks together six across and eight rows down. The outside raw edge of the quilt top is turned under, wrapped around to the back of the quilt and slip-stitched to the backing fabric.

Materials:

Use an assortment of scraps.
Light 4 1/4 yds., Dark 2 3/4 yds.,
Medium 1 1/2 yds.
Each block is made up of 2 units.

Use Templates:

B and *G*.

Quilt Size:

Approximately 72" X 96"

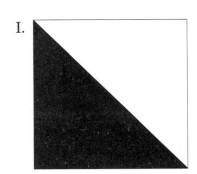

I. Sew one dark *G* to one light *G* (Make 3).

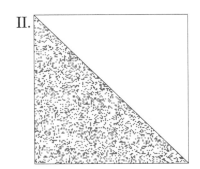

II. Sew one medium *G* to one light *G* (Make 3).

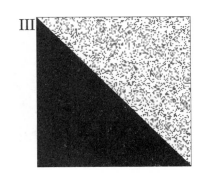

III Sew one dark *G* to one medium *G* (Make 2).

Sew Row 2 as shown in the diagram, making sure of the light and dark orientation of each piece.

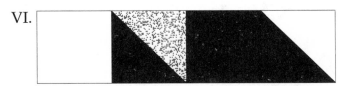

Sew Row 3 according to the above diagram.

Sew Row 4 according to the above diagram.

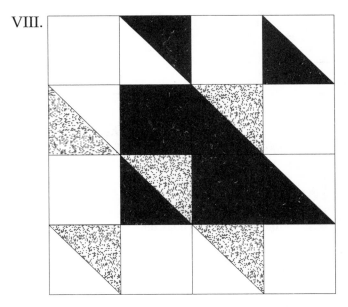

Sew the rows together to complete the block.

IV.

Sew Row 1 as shown in the diagram, making sure the dark and light triangles are turned in the correct orientation.

Pieces per Block:

6 light, 2 dark *B's*; 6 light, 5 medium, and 5 dark *G's*.

Quilt Size:

Approximately 76" X 93"

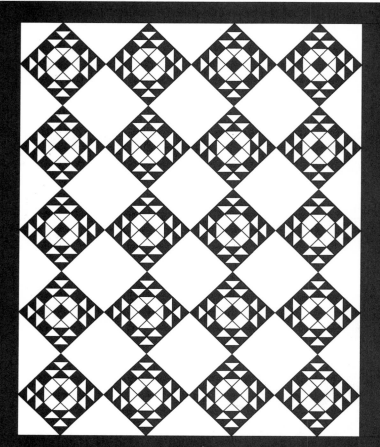

Procedure:

Referring to the block diagrams on the following page, piece 20 blocks. The pieced blocks are set on point four across and five down. 12 1/2" (including seam allowance) solid squares are set between the pieced blocks. Cut the squares with the diagonals along the grain of the fabric. The four corners are 8 1/2" each (add seam allowance). The border is a 4 1/2" strip (including seam allowance) with the length being determined by the size of the finished pieced quilt.

Wedding Ring

Materials:

Use an assortment of scraps.
Light 6 3/4 yds., Dark 2 1/4 yds.
Each block is made up of 2 units.

I.
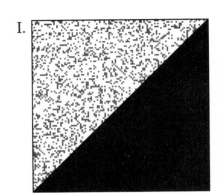
Sew a light *D* to a dark *D* (Make 16).

VI.

Row 5

II.

Sew Row 1 using the above diagram to make sure of the proper orientation of dark and light pieces.

VI.

Complete the block by sewing the rows together beginning with row one.

III.

Row 2

Pieces per Block:

16 light, 16 dark *D's*; 5 light and 4 dark *F's*. Cut twelve plain squares, fourteen half-squares and four corners from light. Cut top and bottom borders and two side borders from light.

IV.
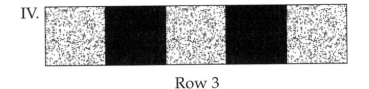
Row 3

V.

Row 4

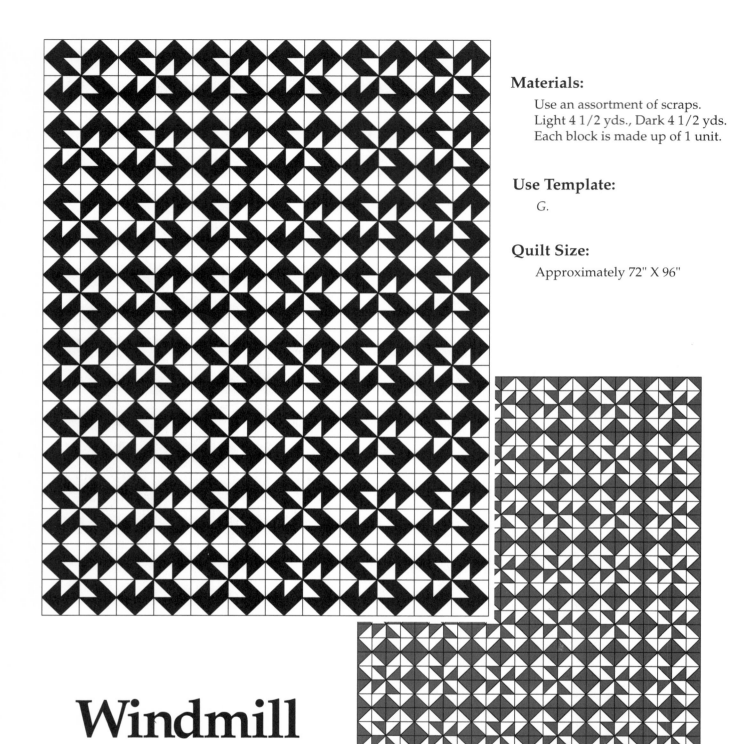

Materials:

Use an assortment of scraps.
Light 4 1/2 yds., Dark 4 1/2 yds.
Each block is made up of 1 unit.

Use Template:

G.

Quilt Size:

Approximately 72" X 96"

Windmill

Procedure:

Referring to the block diagrams on the following page, piece 48 blocks.
Join the blocks together six across and eight rows down. The outside
raw edge of the quilt top is turned under, wrapped around to the back
of the quilt and slip-stitched to the backing fabric.

I.

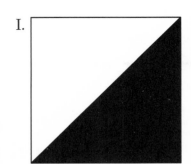

Sew one light *G* to one dark *G* (Make 16).

V.

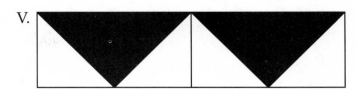

Sew Row 4 according to the above diagram.

II.

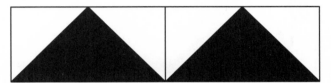

Sew Row 1 using the above diagram to insure that the light and dark pieces are in the correct orientation.

VI.

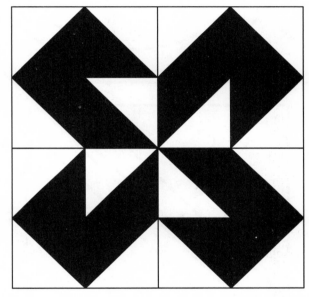

Sew the rows together in order from one to four to complete the block.

III.

Sew Row 2 according to the above diagram making sure of the correct orientation of the pieces.

Pieces Per Block:

16 Light and 16 dark *G's*.

IV.

Sew Row 3 as shown in the diagram, making sure the dark and light triangles are turned in the correct orientation.

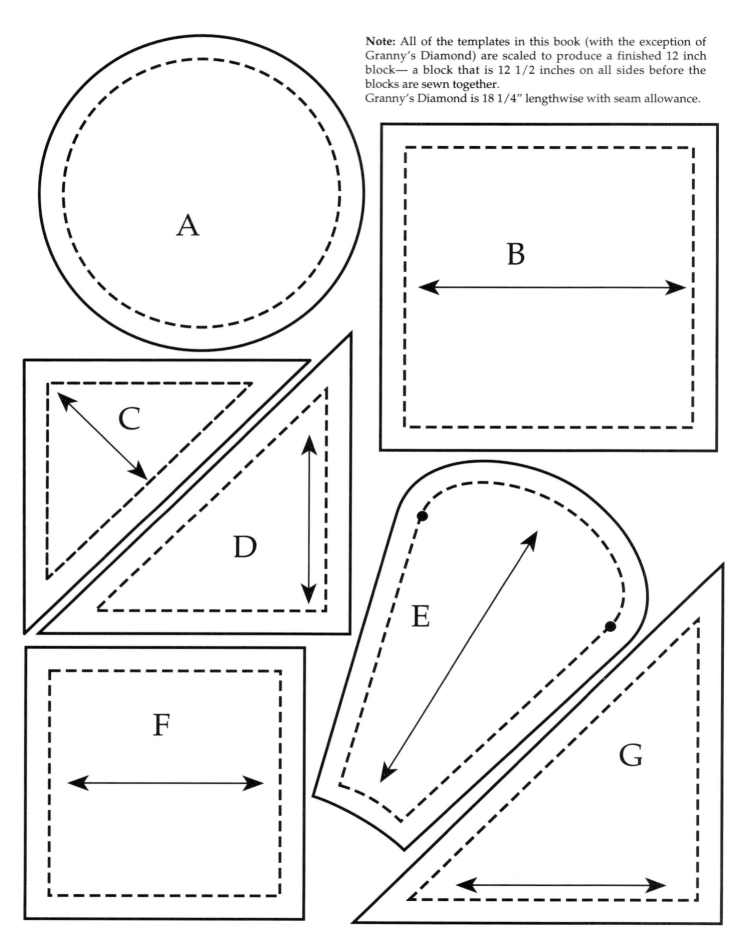

Note: All of the templates in this book (with the exception of Granny's Diamond) are scaled to produce a finished 12 inch block— a block that is 12 1/2 inches on all sides before the blocks are sewn together.

Granny's Diamond is 18 1/4" lengthwise with seam allowance.

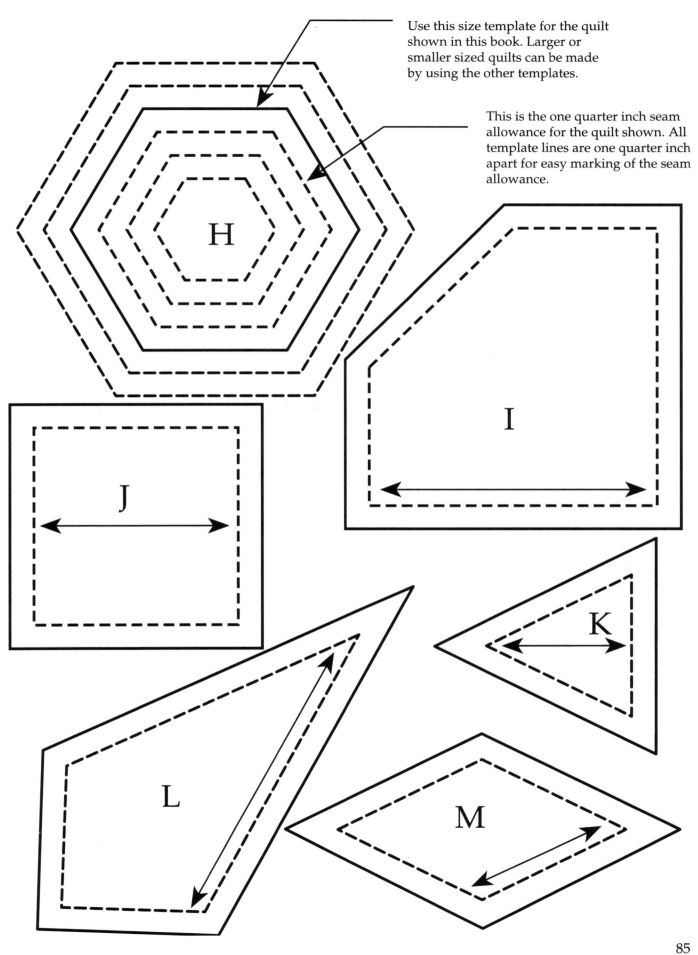

Use this size template for the quilt shown in this book. Larger or smaller sized quilts can be made by using the other templates.

This is the one quarter inch seam allowance for the quilt shown. All template lines are one quarter inch apart for easy marking of the seam allowance.

H

I

J

K

L

M

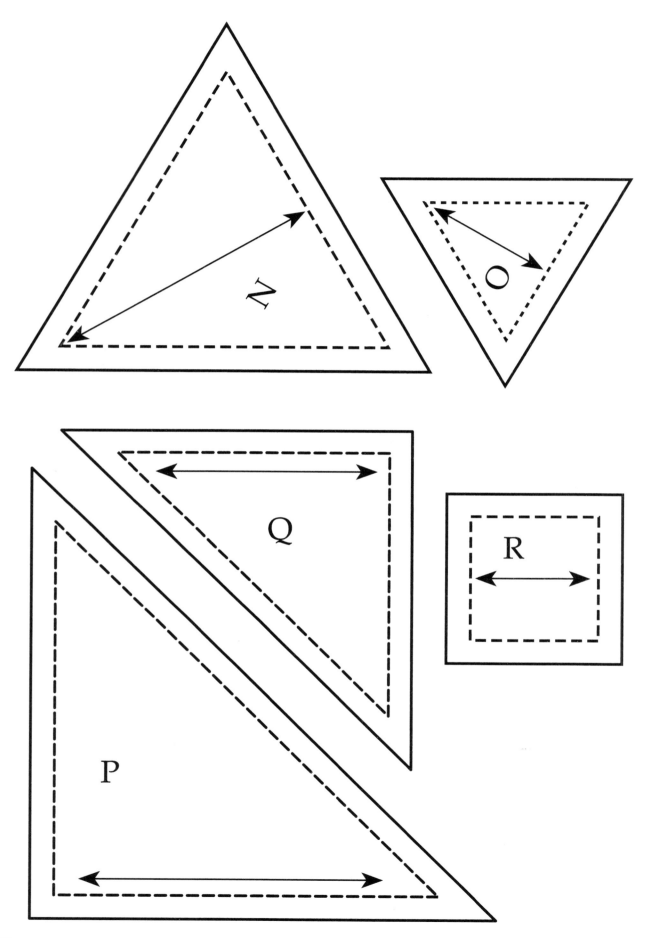

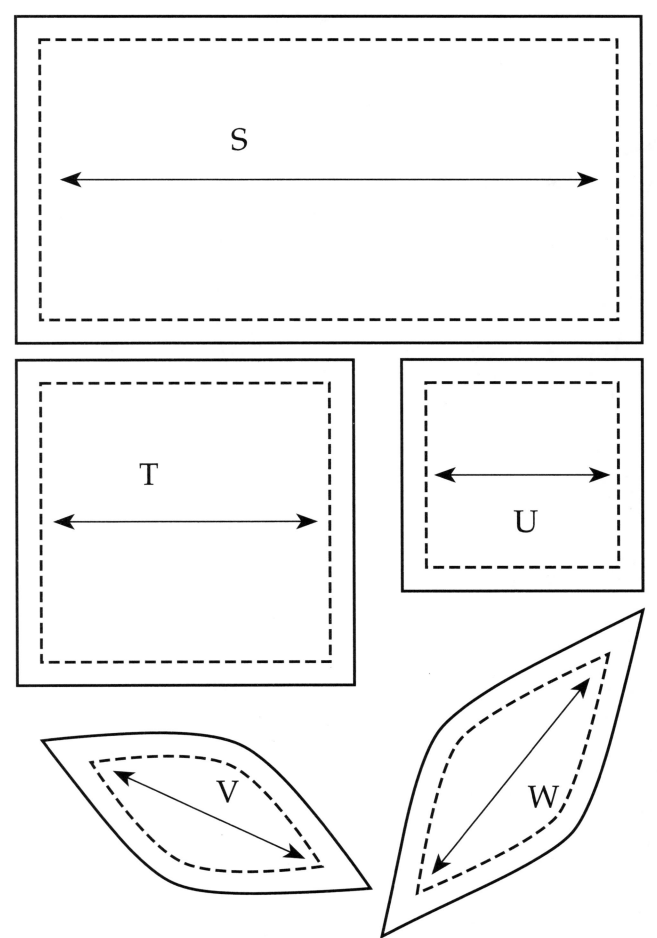

S

T

U

V

W

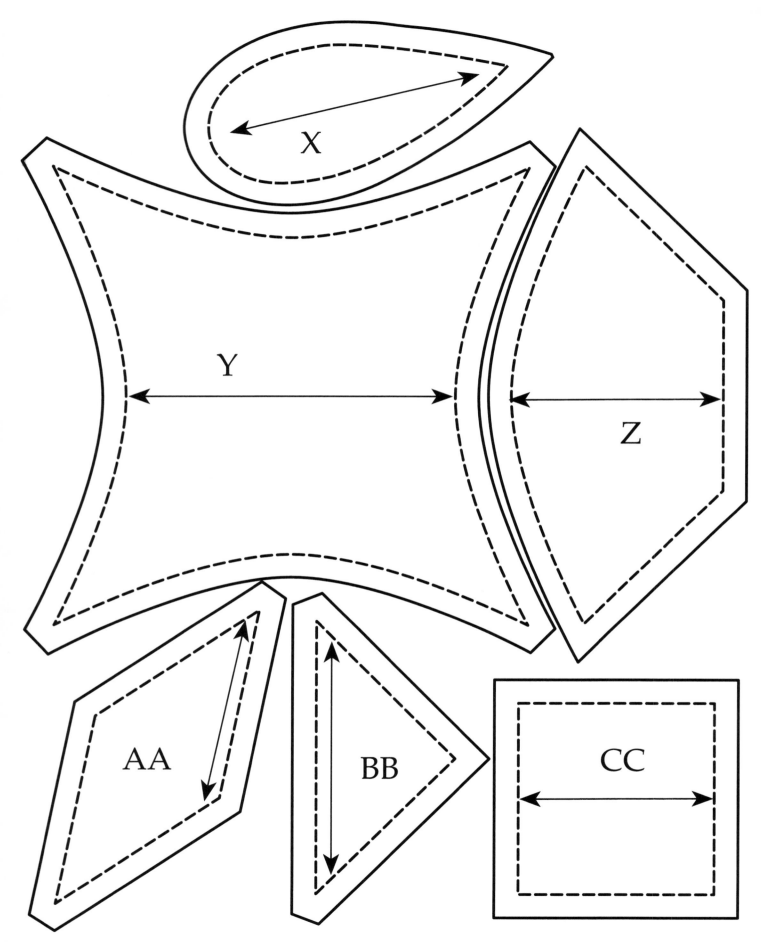

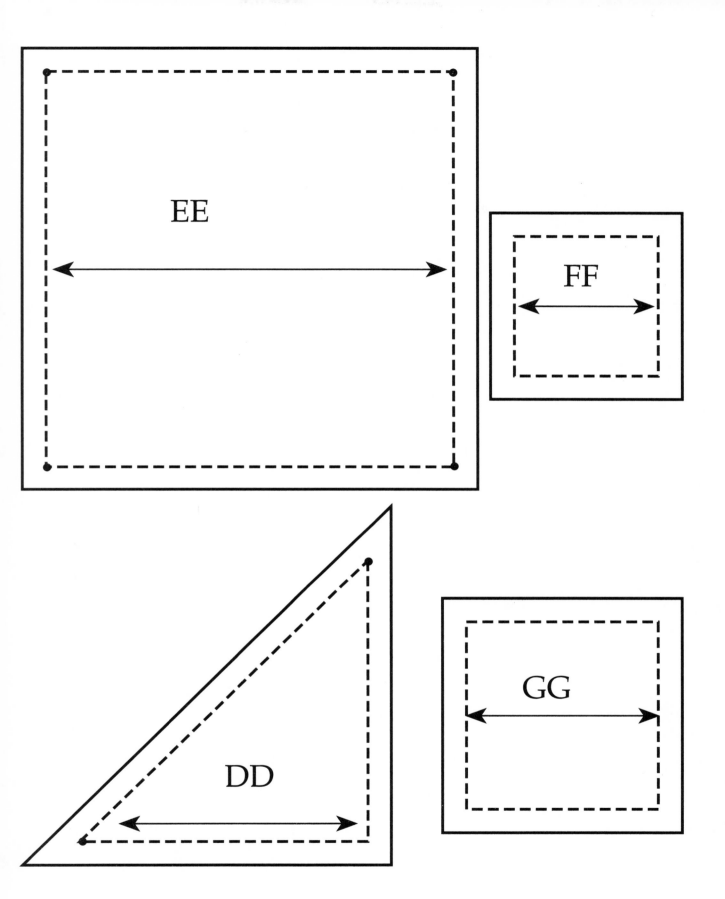

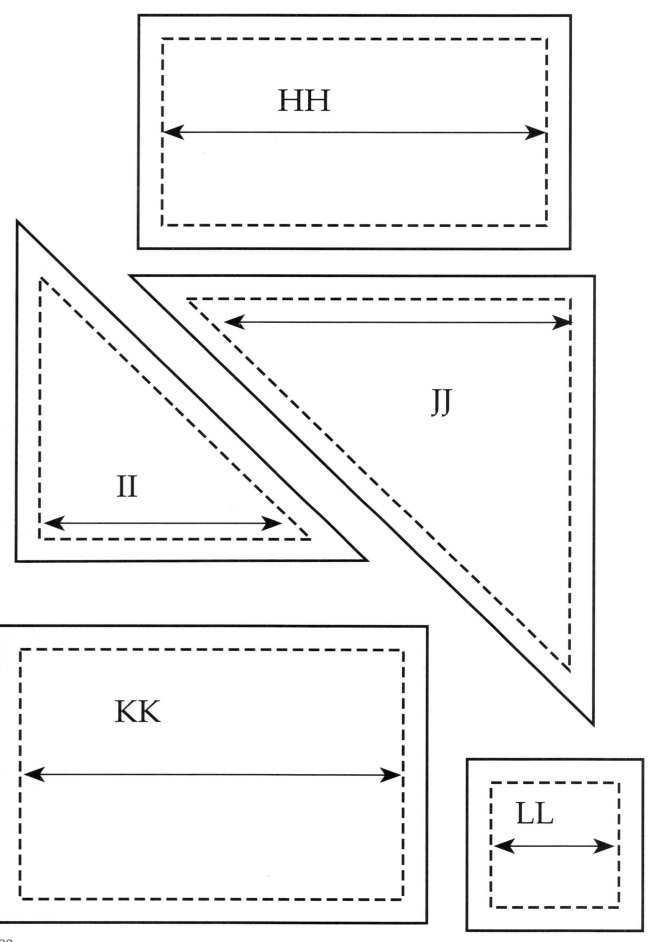

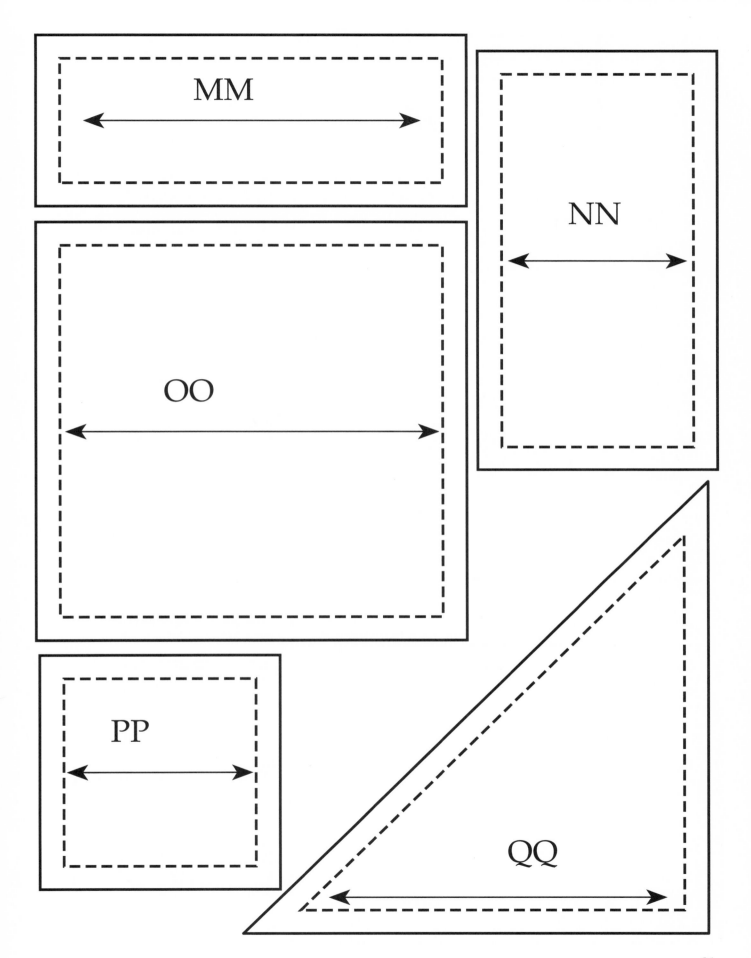

MM

NN

OO

PP

QQ

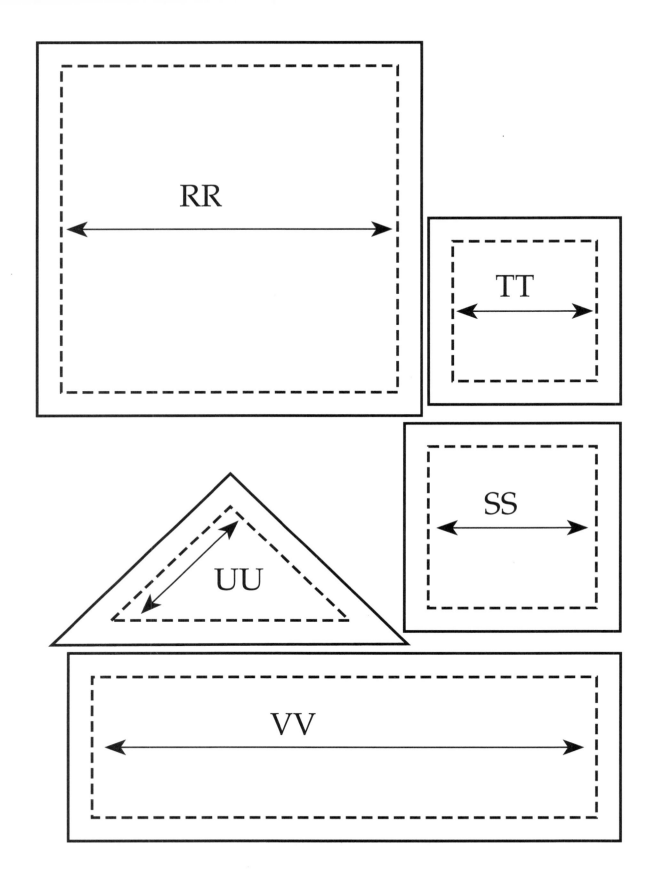

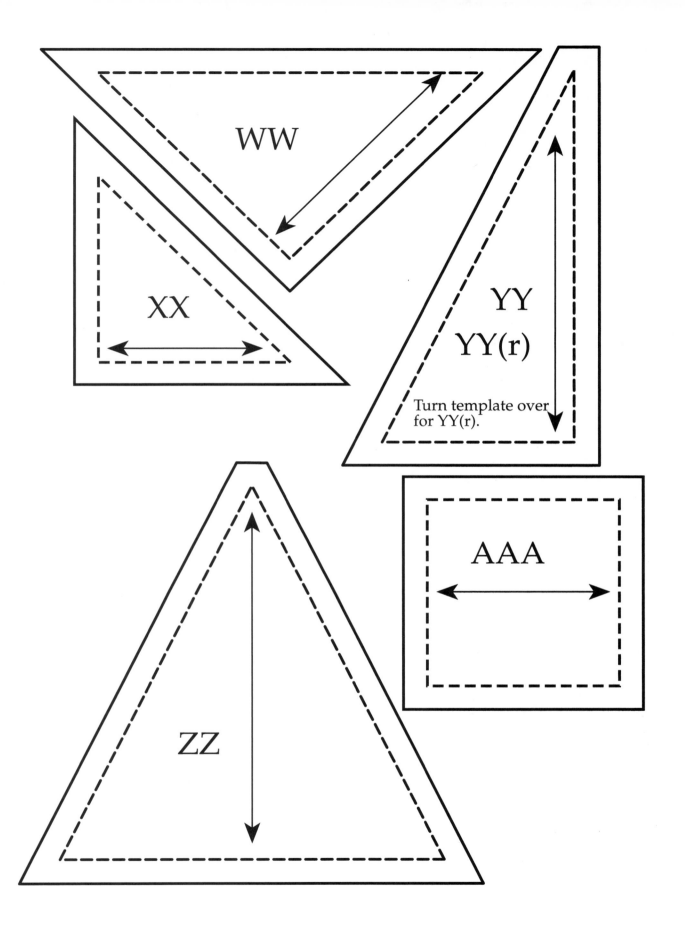

WW

XX

YY
YY(r)

Turn template over
for YY(r).

AAA

ZZ